BUDDHISM & SCIENCE

BUDDHISM & SCIENCE

PAUL DAHLK

TRANSLATED FROM THE GERMAN

BY THE BHIKKHU SILACARA

GYAN

Published by

GYAN

Gyan Publishing House
5, Ansari Road
Daryaganj, New Delhi-110002
Phone: 011-47034999, 9811692060
E-mail: books@gyanbooks.com

Distribution Network
gyanbooks.com
India, USA, Canada, UK, Australia, France

ISBN: 978-81-212-8991-7 (PB)
First Published, 1913

2nd Impression 2023

Printed at: Gyan Press, Delhi.

BUDDHISM & SCIENCE
AUTHOR: PAUL DAHLKE, TRANSLATOR: THE BHIKKHU SILACARA

BUDDHISM AND SCIENCE

MACMILLAN AND CO., LIMITED
LONDON · BOMBAY · CALCUTTA
MELBOURNE

THE MACMILLAN COMPANY
NEW YORK · BOSTON · CHICAGO
DALLAS · SAN FRANCISCO

THE MACMILLAN CO. OF CANADA, LTD.
TORONTO

BUDDHISM & SCIENCE

BY

PAUL DAHLKE

TRANSLATED FROM THE GERMAN

BY

THE BHIKKHU SĪLĀCĀRA

MACMILLAN AND CO., LIMITED
ST. MARTIN'S STREET, LONDON
1913

CONTENTS

INTRODUCTION

The Purpose of the Book

Three kinds of books there are. First, those that give nothing and from which we demand nothing. These constitute the greater portion of the book-world; empty entertainment for the idle. Secondly, those books that give the unfamiliar and are unfamiliar to us—that is, demand only our memory. These are manuals of instruction presenting facts. And thirdly, those books that give themselves and demand ourselves. These are the books that are mental nutriment in the real sense of the words, and impart to the entire process of mental development a stimulus which, like the stimulus imparted to a growing tree, never again can be lost. The present book makes claim to belong to the last category. As something experienced by myself, it is meant to become such an experience to others.

The mental poverty of our time finds its most accurate expression in the prevalent lack of individual experience. We are not impressed where we ought to be impressed, because we allow ourselves to be impressed where in truth there is nothing impressive. We mistake our true interests. The interesting is something in which we have an interest, in which we have a share. But there has been such a derangement of positions that in presence of our true interests we stand stupid spectators, whilst for the interesting in the banal sense, we are ready to go through fire and flood. To the average man of to-day it is far more interesting to read hair-splitting investigations into the question as to whether Christianity is a branch of Buddhism or Buddhism of Christianity, than to think out and live that which both have taught and continue to teach.

All this is inherent in the conditions under which we live at the present time.

Thought is ever confronted by life as by a question—a question that of necessity becomes actual in me, the thinker. For as a candle illuminates a certain portion of space and thereby first calls forth question-raising objects, so does thought itself illuminate these stellar spaces and thereby first calls forth question-raising objects. The *I* is the natural point of departure of every view of the world, being the objective as well as the subjective point of departure. Now that philosophy, in the endeavour to construct a world-conception out of pure thought alone, has come to ruin on her own nothingness, natural science has constituted itself the emissary of the world-conception idea, and in contra-distinction to philosophy has sought to realize it over the head of the *I*, so to speak—an attempt which, despite all its grandeur, is forever doomed to failure, seeing that, as the last to include the *I* itself in this world-theory, the problem is insoluble. Hence the fact that we no longer possess a philosophy such as the ancients and the schoolmen possessed; and do not yet possess a natural science that can give us any genuine aid.

Every thinker, every seeker—and every thinker is a seeker—is to-day in a state of mental interregnum. And it is the hope of this book that, as masses of atmosphere in labile equilibrium frequently at the slightest impulse break into whirling motion, so also the minds of our time that are in this state of labile equilibrium may prove themselves still more susceptible to stimuli, and respond, if not exactly with a mental typhoon, at least with a gentle zephyr.

Three kinds of men there are. First, the indifferent, comparable to the inert bodies of chemistry. To them applies the saying of Confucius, "Rotten wood cannot be turned." Secondly, the believers, comparable to those chemical bodies whose affinities are satisfied. In so far as their faith is genuine, to these applies already during their lifetime, the parable of beggar Lazarus in Abraham's bosom. And thirdly there is the thinking class, destitute of faith, corresponding to chemical bodies in the nascent state. To them applies that word of the Buddha, "Painful is all life."

Our book has value only for this third, last kind. The indifferent, however highly educated he may be, will never give himself the trouble to think it out; and with the believer it will only provoke contradiction.

A thinker destitute of faith I call him who at the idea of endlessness, which none who thinks at all can escape, reacts with that psychic uneasiness which may be compared with the purely intellectual uneasiness one experiences in presence of the irrational in mathematics, both, as a matter of fact, being also analogues.

The circle of readers of this book is thus circumscribed in advance. But the few for whom it is written, they are the few that count.

Three questions there are that before all else occupy every thinking man, and always have occupied him. The question, "What am I?" The question, "How must I comport myself?" The question, "To what end am I here?" This "what," this "how," this "to what end,"—these are the subjects of contention in all mental life. It is not every one who, like Emperor Augustus of old, can withdraw from this scene of things with a *plaudite amici*. There *are* minds to whom life is more than a play, and all that is transient more than a symbol.

It is the negative task of this book to show that neither faith nor science supply such an answer to these questions as can satisfy the thinking man. It is the positive task of this book to show that a solution of these three questions is furnished in the Buddha-thought, but in a form so strange at first sight, that until now it has achieved no practical importance. Trained one-sidedly to inductive attempts at concepts, we know not how to translate into modern prose these enigmatic formulas of thought. We know not what to make of a Nirvana—the epitome of all blessedness and yet no heaven. We know not what to make of a Karma that from beginninglessness binds existence to existence and yet is no soul. And so the truest of all teachings, uncomprehended by philosophy, unheeded by natural science, is lost to us and to the needs of our time.

The question arises, How comes it that Buddhism has always remained essentially alien to us, a sort of mental curiosity?

To this I give the answer, brief and blunt, It is not understood. That is only too painfully evident from the literature published about it. Here I do not at all refer to those commonplace compilations that simply swarm with misconceptions. It is just the best books on the subject which reveal how far removed it is beyond our powers of apprehension.

I am prepared to have reproach brought against me; first, that in many places I have become polemical, and secondly, that I have not sufficiently studied that tone of affected diffidence such as has become the fashion in our books, just in so far as they deal with the theme of a world-conception.

As to the first point, I can bear witness that nowhere have I indulged in polemics for polemics' sake. It is with the Buddha-thought as with many a colossal edifice, whereof the greatness only becomes apparent by comparison with ordinary erections. As in the case of the pyramids of Gizeh, the endless background of the desert offers no fitting standard of measurement for their greatness, so the Buddha-thought, when projected upon beginninglessness alone, offers nothing by which its greatness can be measured. One must place by its side other mental structures if one is ever to be able to reveal it in all its stupendous proportions. It is easy to understand that in this case simple comparison must already amount to polemics.

As to the second point, my opinion is this: Either

one has something useful to contribute, in which case one does not need to practise this affected diffidence, or else one has nothing useful to contribute, in which case one does not need to write at all. I dare speak thus because I bring *nothing of my own*, but only speak in the place of a Greater. "We do not know, but there is no sound reason for doubting that so-and-so," and all such phrases, howsoever couched, by means of which an endlessly considerable probability is intended to be smuggled into the ranks of truth, are quite uncalled for in a teaching like that of the Buddha. Whoso knows, "Thus it is," simply says, "Thus it is."

I

WHAT IS A WORLD-THEORY AND IS IT NECESSARY?

THERE is present a something given, an actuality, which we designate by the collective name of "world." The untutored person and the thinker alike make use of the same expression. This latter is indifferent, acquiring a definite meaning only with reference to a particular explanation—that is, with reference to a view of the world.

The impulse to explain actuality, the need of a world-theory, a world-conception, is deeply embedded in every living being endowed with consciousness.

The moment any being has so far developed as to begin to think, it finds itself involved in a huge system within which it seeks to know its way, striving the while to understand it in its various details.

This system comes before it in a twofold aspect: on the one hand, as "something that is," *i.e.* things; and on the other hand, as "something that happens," *i.e.* the play of events among things. A "being" without a "happening" attached, is as little to be found as a "happening" without a "being." In other words: processes only exist.

Here two questions immediately arise. First, *What is the world?* And second, *How does the play of events come about?*

Both sides of the world-picture, and therewith both questions, blend into one question—the question as to adequate causes. As well the fact that "something is here," as the fact that "something happens," requires adequate causes. *The adequate cause is the thought-necessity given with all mental life.* The entire universe in all its parts and processes, is to the thinking man a species of marionette show. He sees the puppets dance but he does not see the strings, neither does he see that which pulls the strings. The incentive to a view of the world is the craving, so to speak, to get a peep behind the scenes, to spy out Nature's secrets, and therewith seize upon the meaning and significance of life itself. This latter is the real object of every world-theory.

Now it is quite true, that if I do not perceive the meaning and significance of life I am but little better than the donkey that drags the full sacks to the mill and the empty ones back without knowing why, in the one case as in the other. I owe it to my dignity as a man to seek out the meaning and significance of life. But this is not all.

That I am here is a given fact. Were I not here, had I never been here, not for that would any breach have yawned in the structure of the world. But now that I am here, all turns upon *how I conduct myself during this my existence.* Not the fact *that* I am here, but *how* I employ this existence is the all-important thing.

This question as to the "*how*" can only be

answered in any natural way through the "*what.*" I must know what I am, and what are the things and beings outside me; I must learn my relations to the external world, I must apprehend the meaning and significance of life before I can possess a genuine canon and standard for my behaviour, for my morality. For all morality, whether it find expression in doing or in leaving undone, issues in acts of selflessness. This, however, requires that motives be brought forward, otherwise such an act is either a perverted form of self-seeking like all asceticism, or it is mere training, bearing, indeed, the outward semblance of morality, in reality, however, having nothing at all to do with it. It is only in virtue of cognition that any act acquires moral value. One can speak of real morality there only where it is a function of cognition. Hence there can be no morality without comprehension, without a world-conception.

This is the first reason why a world-theory is necessary.

But it behoves a being worthy the name of man also to know whether this life is merely a blind adventure, or whether it has aim and goal. The thinking man demands to know what he may expect after this life. He insists upon looking beyond this life. He claims an answer to the question, "Whence? Whither?"

This demand to look out beyond life, this questioning, as to *the aim and goal of life*, is called *religion.* As with the query, "How must I conduct myself?" which permits of being answered in natural fashion then only when I know what I am, so is it with the question, "Whence am I, and whither am I bound?" Only when I know what I am, can this question also find a natural reply. A genuine religion, like a genuine morality, has its roots in cognition. *Both alike must be functions of cognition.*

Such are the two reasons why for every thinking being a world-theory is not only a matter of giving honourable satisfaction to his dignity as a man, but also why it is a positive necessity. *In their absence genuine morality and genuine religion alike are impossible.*

Now every backward glance into time, *i.e.* universal history, as well as every look round us in space, *i.e.* ethnology, reveals the fact that there never has been, and also that there is not, a people destitute of every trace, every touch of morality and religion. The only question is, Is this natural capacity of mankind for morality and religion a veritable function of cognition?

The essence of all cognition is the individual. Every act of cognition is always something individual, personal, pertaining to me alone. Were all men to cognize alike, the content of this cognition would still be the individual possession of each and every single person. *Cognition separates.*

Opposite to it stands another function of human nature—emotion. *Emotion unites.* If things cognizable are the affair of the individual, things emotional have to do with the mass. Every natural capacity of mankind for morality and religion consists altogether of what pertains to the emotions. Here all morality is founded upon an instinctive feeling of correlation which finds expression in the well-known saying :—

> What you would not men did to you,
> See that you do not them unto!

or in the maxim, "So conduct thyself towards others as thou wouldst wish that they should conduct themselves towards thee!"

The unifying quality of emotion is made manifest in every form of compassion, which latter frequently rises to the pitch of an actual vegetative suffering with the afflicted person. Such facts, open to every one's observation, awaken in all the instinctive feeling of an inner connection of beings, and yield a natural morality that is purely a function of emotion.

It may be asked, "Could such a morality of emotion suffice humanity?"

It would suffice a humanity whose development had only reached so far as the capacity for emotion. So soon, however, as a being passes from the stage of the emotional and enters upon the stage of the cognitive, the morality of emotion no longer suffices, as little so as the reasons one is accustomed to give to children suffice the grown man.

The emotional holds sway as long as an individual is not yet fully conscious of himself, not yet come to pure reflection. So soon as he is fully conscious, there arises also the need to understand ourselves as well as our morality and religion. Then only may I say that I *have* morality and religion when I have understood them, when both have become functions of my cognition. So long as this is not the case, so long are religion and morality things of emotion, and these are subject to every conceivable variation. Hence the endless diversity of moralities as well as of religions in the stage of the emotional.

Here both—to use the language of current speech —are mere matters of taste, lacking in all inner foundation. Hence also comes all that is unintelligible in the manners and customs connected with morality and religion among foreign peoples of ancient and of modern times. This is not the place to go into details. Every historical record, every account of civilization, furnishes abundant examples.

Whether upon our globe a state of affairs has ever prevailed in which morality and religion have been exclusively things of emotion, it is impossible to say. The fact remains that at the point where, in our glance backward over the history of the world, man first emerges, the purity of emotional morality and religion is no longer intact. Historical man, as first presented to us in the states of Egypt and Babylonia, already exhibits a morality and religion which are no longer pure functions of emotion, but have now become functions of reflection.

This necessity for reflection is given with the essential being of all that is real.

As already said, all that is, on the one hand, presents itself as "*something that is*," *i.e.* a being; and, on the other hand, as "something that happens," *i.e.* a becoming; that is, as a process. Wherever something happens, an adequate cause must be present. And the world by its simple existence, by reason of its very nature as a process, is the standing incitement to comprehension, to reflection, inasmuch as the mind hankers after an adequate cause for all that occurs. "The apparent changes in organic being all about me," says Goethe in his *Morphologie*, "took a strong hold of my mind.

Imagination and nature seemed to strive with one another which of the two should stride forward with the bolder and firmer step."

The search after adequate causes is everywhere given as a necessity of thought wherever mental life is found. An adequate cause is required for "that which is," just as much as for "that which happens"; it is that which both presume. *To possess a world-theory and therewith a world-conception means to comprehend adequate causes.*

According to the attitude assumed by mental life toward the question of adequate causes, does it separate off in two main directions: the direction of faith and the direction of science.

II

FAITH AND A WORLD-THEORY

There is present a something given—the world.

It presents itself as an endlessly vast sum of processes. Where there is a process there is happening. Where something happens, there adequate causes are demanded.

Every attempt to comprehend adequate causes leads backwards in endless series, since each cause comprehended is something which itself in turn demands an adequate cause, and so on backwards without ever a conclusion.

Faith is that particular form of mental life which from this fact draws the inference that for the human mind a real comprehension is impossible, since behind the physical there stands a something transcendent, a force, with reference to which all life-phenomena become that which their name expresses: *phenomena of a "life"* which faith for the most part designates by the word "*god.*"

This force stationed behind the physical, to which faith traces back all that happens, must be an "adequate cause in itself," hence something contrary to sense in the fullest meaning of the words. For all that is, without exception, requires an adequate cause. An "adequate cause in itself" would thus be that something which by its simple existence would give the lie to this thought-necessity, inasmuch as itself would be that which would have no adequate cause. When the thought-necessity of an adequate cause is thus satisfied with an "adequate cause in itself," this just means: it is satisfied *in a fashion contrary to sense.*

The essence of all that is contrary to sense consists in this, that when followed out in thought, it deprives itself of the possibility of existence. A mistake in an arithmetical sum is the most familiar form of what is contrary to sense. It is something that in correct thinking is by itself deprived of all possibility of existence; it is something that makes its appearance only that it may appear no more.

In like case stands faith. Does it essay to think that in which it believes, then must that present itself to it in one or other relation or form—that is, conceptually. A transcendent, however, that presents itself conceptually is transcendent no longer, but, on the contrary, the one completely conceptualized thing there is in the world, inasmuch as its whole existence just consists of the concept of it. Accordingly, when faith ventures to think, it deprives itself of the possibility of existence; when it does not think, it has no existence *as faith*, and therefore no existence at all.

When, as in these days frequently happens, people complain of the ever-increasing decay of faith, the reason mostly given is, that faith does not contain a sufficiency of what is of value to the understanding. The believer must know what, how, and why he believes, and not have his faith based simply upon feeling. But this is somewhat the same as if one should reproach darkness with not containing a sufficiency of light among its ingredients. Is light present, then there can be no darkness; is understanding present, then there can be no faith. *Credo ut intelligam* is the most vain of all wishes.

Pantheism in its noblest form, that of the Indian *Vedanta*, endeavours to avoid this dilemma by conceiving of its divine in purely negative terms. But the famous "neti, neti"—"not this, not this"—of the Upanishads, is a definition too, and so a limitation.

Through this its essential characteristic, of itself in being thought out, depriving itself of the possibility of existence, faith takes its place—as third in the trio—along with illusion and error.

Illusion is what I call a mistaken view; *error*, what I call a mistaken experience. When I mistake a rope for a snake, a train of ants for a crack in the ground, these are illusions. When I hold infusoria to have their origin in the infusion of hay, or look upon the evening and the morning star as two different orbs, these are errors.

Upon this, its community of nature with illusion and error, is based another essential characteristic of faith—namely, the impossibility, when once it has vanished, of its ever again coming to life. Once the rope on my path which I formerly mistook for a snake has been recognized by me for a rope, never again can I voluntarily return to my illusion. I can, indeed, by force of imagination, represent it to myself as a snake, but this representation no longer "works"; it no longer excites fear. And in just the same way I can quite successfully recall the conditions under which certain optical and acoustic delusions made their appearance, but they are illusions that are dead. The like holds good of error and, for a third, of faith.

People who call for a resuscitation of vanished faith, and by some means or other hope to see it effected, know not what it is that they hope and call for. They are calling for the restoration of a vanished ignorance—an utter inconceivability.

Now there exists one great distinction between faith, on the one hand, and illusion and error on the other; in this respect, namely, that the two latter have the physical, the material for their object, hence can be checked and set right by this—that is, by reality. Faith, however, that has for its object the non-physical, the non-material, which is just whatever the believer chooses to conceive it to be, cannot be checked and set right by reality. On the contrary, the believer interprets the entire world in accordance with his concept, devours, so to speak, the world's entire content of reality, and sets up a view of the world that is *unreal,* seeing that he interprets the physical from the transcendental standpoint—that is, abnormally; and therefore he is never in the position to be set right by reality, since he never can knock up against contradictions. One must know that one does not know before one can let oneself be taught.

In perfect accordance with this essential feature of faith (so far as the theory of knowledge is concerned) is its morality and religion: *both are contrary to sense.*

The essence of all morality is to be found in selflessness. Every act of selflessness requires a motive. To possess a motive one must exercise cognition, comprehension.

As a matter of fact the essential nature of every faith-morality is selfish, despite all its acts of renunciation. Here one practises renunciation like a man who stints himself of a certain amount of money and invests it in a lottery. As he parts with his money that he may win back more in its place, so here the believer gives up money, goods, life—yea, honour and truth, everything, if so be he may draw the first prize above.

The essence of all religion consists in the search for the aim and goal of life. This search faith satisfies by referring life as a whole to a something transcendent. But the existence of the transcendent is nothing else but the concept of it. To refer life as a whole to a transcendent thus means nothing but to refer itself to itself, which—so to speak—is the analytical expression for ignorance.

Further development of these ideas is not essential to our task. Here we have only to bear well in mind that, as the world-theory from the standpoint of faith is one contrary to sense, so also is its morality and its religion. All three are functions of a nescience, and therefore void of actuality.

III

SCIENCE AND A WORLD-THEORY

THERE is present a something given—the world.

With reference to this something given, science takes up a position that in its own way is every whit as arbitrary as again in its way is that of religion ; with this difference, however, that whereas the latter, so to speak, turns the clock of mental life backward, science would fain turn it forward.

The play of world-events with equal justice may be held to declare that we comprehend adequate causes as to declare that we do not comprehend them, inasmuch as all we may have comprehended as the adequate cause of any life-phenomenon, itself on its part demands an adequate cause, and so on backwards *ad infinitum.* In short, Every adequate cause is of a secondary nature. From this science argues as follows :—

It is a fact that we comprehend adequate causes, in certain respects, up to a certain degree, consequently perfect comprehension is possible, everything depending simply on patience and correct methods.

With this claim of the *comprehensibility in principle* of life-phenomena, science takes upon itself the proud task, of itself *working out a world-theory* from the foundation upwards

Comprehensibility in principle of life-phenomenon is that standpoint with reference to actuality which is given for every science without exception. On any other hypothesis science as science has no justification whatever for its existence. Science, if it is to be what its name implies, is that which furnishes knowledge. Knowledge can only be furnished where things can be completely demonstrated, made tangible to sense. That, however, is only possible if nothing lies hidden in things that is not perceptible by sense. Hence science, if she does not wish to gainsay her own right to exist, must proceed upon the arbitrary hypothesis that *there is nothing in the play of world-events that is not perceptible to the senses.* And if really there is something of the sort there, then for her it is merely the *not yet demonstrable*, which later on, with patience, with improvements in methods, will also be achieved. This is the position which science takes up with reference to the play of world-events, the foundation on which her whole superstructure is erected. Science is possible there only where there is the sensible, the demonstrable, where there is something so constituted that I can class it with others of its kind. And all science—to put it briefly—is just the endeavour to make tangible to sense the entire play of world-events.

In support of this standpoint in principle of science, I cite the following passage from W. Ostwald's *Schule der Chemie*:—

Pupil. These are only properties. What I mean, however, is that which lies at the root of all properties.

Teacher. This then ought to remain behind when you

have thought away all properties from the matter. Well, think away all its properties from a piece of sugar—colour, shape, hardness, weight, taste, and so forth—what then remains over? Nothing! For it is only through its properties that I can recognize that there is something there. . . . You must get rid of the notion that apart from the properties of a thing there is anything at all to be found beneath them that is higher or more real than the properties.

From this rejection of all that is not perceptible to sense, it follows that science may not recognize as adequate causes for "that which is" even as for "that which happens"—in short, for all the phenomena of life—anything else but other phenomena of life. If for faith the thought-necessity, an adequate cause, becomes an "adequate cause in itself," *a pure absolute*, for science it becomes *a pure relative*. Anything is an adequate cause purely in its relation to another phenomenon of life, and with reference to itself another phenomenon of life again is the adequate cause. In brief, the adequate cause is here just as much an "effect" as a "cause."

With this rejection in principle of all that is not perceptible to sense, science rejects all actual energies. For *an actual energy can never be anything perceptible to sense*, the latter ever and always necessitating the question as to its adequate cause.

In the universe as constructed for itself by science, the actuating impulse is simply the various differences that obtain in situation and tension, which are equally as countless in number as the countless processes with which they are given. The play of world-events in its entirety becomes a stupendous process of compensation, and all values become simply values of relation. Here nothing has sense and meaning by itself, but only as it first receives them from others.

The purely scientific standpoint can only be the materialistic one, along with which of necessity is given the mechanical mode of apprehending the play of world-events.

In the mechanical apprehension of things, the play of world-events becomes a "falling." Every fall demonstrates the absence of actual forces by the fact that in its downward course it can be computed in advance.

The aim and object of all science is computation in advance. The ability to do this finds its due expression in scientific *law*.

The proof that upon this path one had arrived at a world-theory, would thus be an absolutely and universally valid law.

Such a law science does not possess. Every law, without exception, is an abstraction from experience, and may be swept away again by fresh experiences.

Now it is true modern physics lays claim to one universal law—the law of the conservation of energy.

We shall have to return to this law later on. Here in passing be it only said—

First, That the law of the conservation of energy has by no means been arrived at upon the legitimate path of science—that is, upon the path of induction—but has been found intuitively. Secondly, The law of the conservation of energy is nothing but a "reading" of the facts, on one hand, by way of definite compromise; on the other, valid only for a limited domain of nature.

The compromise is as follows:—

Were the law of the conservation of energy really a law abstracted from experiences and absolutely valid, it would be proven by the complete passing over, without any remainder, of one phenomenon of life into another; as, for instance, by the transformation of a process of heat into a process of motion; and physics would have a right to draw the conclusion of an analogy between this and other processes. The play of world-events as pure relation-values, its potential comprehensibility, would be proven by a single transformation without residue, of heat into motion and motion back into heat—that is, by a single *completely reversible process.*

But the idea of reversible processes has practical and theoretical possibility only in an absolutely closed system. Such a thing, however, is not to be had in the world of actuality. All things here, without exception, stand in relation to one another, and these mutual relations do not admit of total suspension even for a single moment of time. Thus at no time can one get anything but approximately closed systems; therefore at no time can one attain to anything but approximately correct results. Every attempt to demonstrate practically a completely reversible process works with minimum losses, which the physicist, to be sure, lays to the charge of the procedure adopted, but which the thinker is equally justified in interpreting as a *loss* of energy. No matter what the exactitude with which the experiment is carried out, no matter how small in value the loss, it is always there; *there is no such thing as a completely reversible process!* One can only derive a law of the conservation of energy from the facts, if for thought the same is already given. From experiments alone, inductively, it would be as impossible to arrive at a law of the conservation of energy as it would be to arrive at the concept of the circle solely from the concept of the polygon. The circle must be given beforehand as ultimate concept (*Grenzbegriff*); and in exactly the same way the law of the conservation of energy must be given beforehand as ultimate concept (*Grenzbegriff*), if the experiments are to lead up to it. Thus it was with Robert Mayer's great intuition: it was a thing given. And this intuition was taken up by science and worked out, because here was given it a means of proving with scientific appliances the impossibility of a *perpetuum mobile*. Perpetual motion, however, is the violation of the law of adequate cause, transferred to the domain of the physical.

That is one side of the matter. The other is that the law of the conservation of energy conformable with its nature, can only possess validity in the domain of processes reversible and not dependent upon time, for in a non-reversible process there would lie no possibility whatever of its proof.

Here this is quite enough to signalize the nature of the law of the conservation of energy. In the conception of the play of world-events as yielded by this law, the physicist turns his eyes entirely away from the real, active energies of the play of world-events. He confines himself entirely to what is exhibited to sense, the motions; he takes them for the forces themselves, but is entitled to do so only so long as he keeps clear before him the fact that it is only a *reading* that is in question, and derives therefrom what alone can be derived—*work done*. Work done, however, is not energy itself but the reaction from energies. And that which the physicist calls the "world-picture of energetics" is, in point of fact, void of all energies. The entire world-picture of energetics is no *actual* thing but, in the strictest sense, a thing *re-actual*,—if such a word may be coined—which as such has no title whatever to be used as a world-theory. Should, nevertheless, this occur, then those consequences follow about which we shall speak later.

So long as science abides by actuality she can say nothing else but that every attempt to trace back completely one phenomenon of life to another—that is, to represent the play of world-events in the form of pure relation-values—slips into an endless series; and what is most of all worthy of remark, each member of this endless series is itself in turn the point of departure for a new endless series, so that in the last analysis the fact of this limitless comprehensibility of the phenomena of life remains as the one real problem of science. And every science that is in earnest, and does not merely seek to avail itself of technique, at the very outset must ask itself the question, This limitless onward movement which every point of departure yields, start where we may, has it or has it not a conclusion?

To be able to judge of that one must possess some firm standing-ground from which to look out and see whether this unceasing progression really is progress. On this journey upon the high seas of knowledge one must have a landmark by which to steer. Such a possibility, however, is excluded, and excluded by science itself. For, as already said, science as such has standing only where the hypothesis of potential comprehensibility, of the absence of all that is not perceptible to sense holds good; in other words, where the play of world-events admits of being resolved without remainder into relation-values. Such a landmark, however, could only be something which itself did not admit of being resolved into pure relation-values, but was a constant in itself, an unconditioned constant. Were science, however, to admit the existence of such a "something," she would be cutting the ground from under her own feet. The whole value of science, as such, resides in its pure relativity, in the liability of its values; even as the value of faith resides in the fixity of its one value.

From all this it follows that in science itself absolutely nothing can be found that might serve it to prove whether or not there is genuine progress toward knowledge—that is, whether all these endless series, which every experiment and every piece of thought opens up, do or do not proceed toward a final conclusion. At this stage one view of the matter has precisely as much justification as the other; an *ignorabimus* just as much and just as little value as the most flamboyant optimism. We cannot know. It is, so to speak, entirely a matter of taste as to the sense in which one chooses to interpret these endless series.

In full consonance with this is the value which science possesses in relation to morality and religion.

Whoso will give mankind morality and religion,

must give it something in which it can find support. Both morality and religion at bottom are nothing but a support in the wide waste of infinitudes. Every thinking man craves for such a support. If it is lacking, then for the real thinker a condition supervenes that is all as unbearable as that physical one, when for the moment a person has lost all possibility of learning the lie of his surroundings, as, for instance, when he wakes up confused out of a deep sleep and does not know how to find his way anywhere. Here as there it is the pure anguish of thought that comes over us in such a condition, an anguish that will not let us rest until we have again constructed the mental support, again established continuity in thought with the whole.

If faith fabricates this support in a manner contrary to sense, and consequently projects in consonance with her nature a morality and religion that are contrary to sense, science as a whole on its part is nothing but the attempt to fabricate for itself a support in law. Scientific law, however, yields a support solely with reference to a theory of knowledge. Hence never under any circumstances can science project moral and religious values. It would be a contradiction of her own nature. Could she do so, she would no longer be science—*i.e. the* form of mental life which *must* comprehend the entire play of world-events in the form of relation-values. Where there exists nothing but relation-values, there can exist no support in itself, and therefore no morality or religion. Science is *a-moral* and *a-religious*; and the layman as well as the scientist himself ought ever to keep this clearly before his mind. The efforts made in our day to carve out, so to speak, the results of science to suit religious ends as modern monism seeks to do, only go to show how necessary is such an admonition. From the continuity of life, expounded in the materialistic sense as a cell, men seek to deduce the idea that we ourselves live on in the generations to come, somewhat as the manure lives on in the plant it has manured. But these are such playthings of thought as only are possible where one is operating with what is wholly divorced from actuality, that is, with the empty concept of "life."

To seek to derive moral and religious values from science is, as the Indian saying has it, "to milk the bull by the horns."

Now both faith and science alike have the same starting-point—the thing given, the world. The question then arises, "How can it be possible that with reference to this given thing, each should take up such a directly opposite position? How comes it that the one apprehends the adequate cause of the play of world-events as a pure absolute, while the other apprehends it as a pure relative?"

At this point we come face to face with the Buddha-thought and its significance for mental life.

IV

AN INTRODUCTION TO THE THOUGHT-WORLD OF THE BUDDHA GOTAMA

As aid towards a better understanding of that personality of the greatest significance for the mental life of mankind, there follow here some remarks upon him and the age in which he lived.

Buddhism is the teaching of *the Buddha*, or as one may equally well say—of *the Buddhas*. For "Buddha" is no private name, but the title of one endowed with certain mental capacities. The word, therefore, ought always to be accompanied by the article. It signifies, The Awakened.

According to the teaching the number of the Buddhas is endless. He whom we know by this name, for the time being the last of this beginningless series, is the Buddha Gotama. His family name was *Siddhattha.* He came of the ancient race of the Sakyas, well known for their pride, and as such belonged to the warrior caste. He is, therefore, often alluded to under the name of "Sakyaputta," scion of the Sakyas, or as "Samaṇa Gotama," ascetic Gotama.

He was born in *Kapilavatthu*, the capital city of a small state in Northern India, on the borders of present-day Nepal. His grave was discovered in the year 1898 near Pipravā, in the jungle-covered foothills of the Himalayas called the Terai.

The years of his birth and of his death cannot be exactly determined. Meanwhile one does not go far wrong if one places the period of his activity in the neighbourhood of the year 500 before the Christian era. This would make him the elder contemporary of Heraklitus of Ephesus and somewhat younger than Lao Tse in China.

He died at the advanced age of eighty years (if one does not choose to regard the recurring statements in the texts as to age, on the part of the most different personalities, as merely an indication of old age in general), after almost fifty years of active life spent in travelling about, preaching.

The precepts, discourses, and explanations—all that which makes up the Buddhist canon—are gathered together into what is called the *Tipitaka*, or *Three Baskets*. The language of the canon is Pāḷi. Whether this was the Buddha's own mother tongue or only related to it, is a question upon which there exist differences of opinion between native and European scholars.

The mental atmosphere in which the Buddha arose may be briefly characterized as follows: A feeling of life as suffering, fermenting throughout the entire Indian people; a firm belief in the *transmigration of the soul* and the endless prolongation of this suffering conditioned thereby; the conviction that asceticism purifies, after the effected purification from old guilt, heaps up merit, assures re-birth in heaven, and finally procures deliverance from *Samsara*, this terrible, ceaseless wandering from existence to existence. Once more, the fundamental theme in this Indian symphony of destiny, recurring in unending variations, was this, *Life is Suffering*, or to say the least of it, a somewhat doubtful blessing. But this statement of life as suffering was not in ancient India the hollow phrase that it is with us to-day; neither was it that cold play of thought found in many philosophical systems. It was a grim reality which men sought to escape with an energy of self-immolation, a determination, a recklessness, an ardour of which we lukewarm creatures of to-day can form no conception.

India in the days of the Buddha was full of companies of monks and schools of ascetics, all of them wrestlers with the riddle of life. But one only wrestles with life when one feels it as suffering.

The sons of noble families left their homes to search for truth either out there in the frightful solitudes of the Indian forest, or in the cloister of the monk. As in later days men went forth in search of El Dorado, so in those days did men go forth upon the search for truth. But what gives to the search for truth in ancient India a character entirely its own is this, that all search here is turned towards the *I* itself; that the fight for truth did not as in ancient Greece exhaust itself in elegant rhetorical disputations and exercises in dialectic, but in full unmitigated rigour was lived out in one's own *I*, without a single thought as to whether the outward form would support the heat of the friction within or not.

Amid this swarm of searchers for truth the young Siddhattha also made his appearance. "Black-haired, in the bloom of manhood," in spite of weeping and wailing parents, in spite of a loved and loving wife, in spite of a dear young son, he left his father's halls where he had led a life of rarest pomp and pleasure to enter shaven of head and garbed in yellow, upon the inclement life-path of the penitent. It was the force of thought that drove him forth. He gazed face to face on the transiency of all that lives, and troubled, tormented by this irresistible, unseizable flood of appearances, he turned his mental eye inwards, resolved to find there in the depths of his own *I* that hold and stay which the outer world everywhere denied to him, the weary. Truthfulness toward oneself, seriousness of search regardless of consequences, an unfailing sense of reality, that was the foundation upon which that most banal of all phrases, adapted as is no other to coquetting with itself—the phrase, "All is transient," —became for him that unique teaching of which he himself could say with ample right, "It is the teaching which is founded upon itself."

In one of the Buddhist monk's chants there occurs the phrase, "One single thing—he thinks it out!" This, in few words, is what the Buddha did. He thought out to an end, *one* thought—the thought of transiency. I will not call his teaching the grandest or the deepest of all teachings. Grand, likewise, is Heraklitus's teaching of the All-becoming; deep, likewise, is the Vedanta teaching of the All-one in Brahman; but the teaching of the Buddha is more than this—*it is actual.* Through this it obtains that really compelling character such as is possessed by actuality alone. For there is only one thing that is compelling—truth; and there is only one thing that is true—actuality.

Through this its truthfulness, his teaching has conquered half a world; not by fire and sword but even as truth conquers, by demonstration, by teaching. And so it now stands, old by two thousand years, before the portals of western culture, and claims entrance not into the cloudy domain of a vague mysticism or a crude pantheism, but into the realm of clear, clean thinking, as fulfilment of that which never can be attained by the means at the disposal of science. Comprehension, a world-conception, this goal of all mental life, made impossible by science in its false apprehension of the task—this the Buddha resolves in the limitation that reveals the genius.

Whoso, if only from afar, has scented the import of the Buddha and his teaching, must feel that here he has to do with something wholly unique. One can place on one side not only all the religions of the world but also all the philosophical and scientific systems, and upon the other Buddhism will take its place alone. Yet not as their antithesis. Buddhism is the teaching of actuality, and actuality has no antitheses, because itself the union of antitheses. The Buddha laid hold of actuality there where alone it can be laid hold of—in one's own *I*. Here he found the secret law, the sacred riddle that the chorus outside there mockingly sings us, like to some oracle of Delphi at one and the same time revealing and concealing.

All religions founded upon revelation are of a decidedly revolutionary nature. Buddhism is a pure evolution, a process of mental development in which thought, so to speak, passes a culminating point and works on with reversed signs. This reversal of all life-values has set in with a new point of view, from which the *struggle for no more existence*, so unintelligible for us, follows as a logical necessity. Henceforth truth is no more the servitor of life, but life of truth. As a candle manifests itself through itself, by consuming itself in burning, so does the *I* manifest itself through itself in expending itself in thinking. In this teaching he is not great who loves most, but he who thinks most.

The full scope of this can only be understood later; for the moment it may serve the reader as preparation for what is to follow. Let him know then, at the very outset, that here he enters the realm of a man who seeks not life but truth—a man for whom life has no value in itself but only as an instrument of truth. Him I call a sorry seeker for truth who in his investigation of the riddle of life, sets life itself as sacrosanct in a place of security, making that which is to be measured into the measure itself.

To unite in passion, to contrive clever arrangements that insure the success of the business of propagation and the rearing of the young generation, these the animals also can do; their arrangements for living together in herds are by far more ingenious than those of men; but the capacity to doubt, to question, to seek—of these even the most highly developed animals possess only faint suggestions.

To doubt is the duty of man, and the Buddha is the representative type of humanity, because *the* doubter. We common men, we do indeed doubt of this and of that, and pique ourselves in no small measure upon our powers of judgment; but we none of us get any further than the symptoms. He alone seized at one grasp the entire, ever-changing host of doubts and questions by the root, with the daring of genius demanding to know the right to exist of life itself. This the reader ought well to bear in mind, otherwise for him the Buddha-thought must always retain something strange and forbidding, even as for the honest townsman we all know, a man who dares go up to High Authority Itself—whether established in heaven or on earth—and ask for its identification papers, ever remains in some sort a fear-inspiring figure.

I now pass on to a point more external, but one, none the less, that has its own importance in an introduction to the thought-world of the Buddha.

Buddhism is not only the oldest of the three world-religions, but also the only one of the three that is of Aryan origin.

The significance of this fact lies for me not in the racial question, but in the matter of language. The tongue in which the Buddha preached, taught, and thought, whether it was the Pāḷi itself or some dialect related to it, belongs to the Indo-Germanic stem. The root-words, the grammatical constructions, are akin to those found in European languages. Without any more said, we see how deep is the tie that binds us to the Buddha. Mental life can mix and blend with mental life only through the medium of language. If no congruity exists between one language and another, neither can there be any congruity of thought. We know what enormous difficulties block the way of any European scholar who would force an entrance into the thought-world of the Chinese. So much so, that even at this late day it is still possible to argue the point as to whether the Chinese have any conception of deity at all. To this day it remains open to every translator to interpret Lao Tse, for example, either as a "god-inspired man"—to quote a good Christian translator—or as a free-lance in the fields of thought.

Something similar, if in somewhat less positive terms, may be advanced concerning the Semitic stem. Who can say whether the Indo-German has ever rightly understood Semitism as the deserts of Judea and Arabia have hatched it out. The absurdities and confusions of thought in which Indo-German peoples find themselves entangled the moment they make the attempt to understand and think it out leave it fairly open to doubt. It may be, that pure Semitism, that is to say, that flat contradiction to sound sense, a personal god, can only be perfectly digested with the help of the Semitic root language. The thinking of the Indo-Germanic peoples, or rather of the Indo-Germanic root language, has set itself against this bald crudity from the very beginning. At the idea of predestination, over which the Semite Paul balances his way with considerable natural agility, the half-Aryan Augustine only comes to grief. For the brutality with which the latter champions this dogma is nothing else but the expression of the brutality with which he forcibly squeezed his own mind beneath its yoke. For us the Aryan speaking and thinking, a religion that in its natural logical consequences conducts to such an anomaly as predestination, is either at bottom a moral monstrosity, and so incapable of becoming religion, or else it is a thing misunderstood.

On the other hand, I should refer the intellectual derailment which the Buddha-thought has undergone in Tibet, China, and Japan, in no small measure to the lack of congruity that exists between the Indo-German and the Mongolian languages. The tongue of the Mongol is simply incapable of rendering exactly the content of the Pāḷi syllables.

Buddhism is the teaching of actuality, and its language also—the Pāḷi—as regards content of actuality, takes a leading place among languages.

As upon one hand one may look upon the phenomena of life as processes, actualities, things alive, and upon the other as things rounded off in themselves, rigid, strictly defined, realities, according as, following mental disposition, here the one there the other mode of comprehension predominates, so in one language does the thrust of the actual predominate, and in the other the thrust of the real, the objective. In the one the *dynamic* predominates, in the other the *static*.

A language of an eminently static character is the Latin; whence the impossibility of finding another equally good to take its place in a well-ordered *corpus juris*, with which latter capacity for definition counts above everything. What jurisprudence requires is the complete, the bounded (objectively as well as conceptually) realities. It lops away everything actual, which at all times and places is a *processive motion*, a species of *status nascens*, until comprehended it can be grasped, pretty much as out of the actual surface of the earth in a state of constant transformation the land-surveyor cuts out a piece, settles it as something real and seizable, so that as such its owner at will can exchange it, till the time when the millenium hand on the horologe of the world indicates an advance and renders necessary a new settlement, a new definition. This method is quite sufficient where it is only a question of arriving at definite ends. It corresponds to that which in another place was styled the *re-actual* comprehension of things, and the Latin word *res*, considered etymologically, points directly to this "re-actual" feature.

In complete opposition to Latin the Pāḷi is a language of an eminently actual character. The seeming offences against logic, that with more or less good nature have been laid to the charge of the Buddha by western scholars, have their rise in this content of actuality that distinguishes the language on one hand and its thinking on the other. In actuality there is nothing defined or definable to be found—nothing but a relentless processive movement. Every definition is a compromise with actuality, and is always to be held, as such, by every genuine thinker.

It is owing to this content of actuality in Buddhism and its language that so many expressions are found in it for which a fitting translation is scarcely or not at all to be found. In language, also, a gradual stiffening process is taking place amongst us which renders us ever more capable in definition, and ever more incapable in the comprehension of actuality. Here quite evidently we are caught in a vicious circle. We are proud of this our ability in defining, and imagine we have comprehended the thing itself when we have succeeded in decorating it with a definition. In such cases, however, all we have really done is to fling bridges of thought, as it were, high up over things, which permit us to hop from one conceptual "place" to another without once wetting even our toes in actuality. On the Rhine near Bonn there stands hewn in stone these words: "Caesar primus flumini pontem imposuit." There are not a few minds associated with the lecture-room and laboratory who take themselves for Cæsars when they "impose" new definitions upon things, upon actuality. The riddles of life in this wise are neatly and perfectly resolved in definitions; which, after all, is nothing very much to wonder at with riddles of life that for the most part only exist in the form of definitions.

All things in the world are so constituted that with them concept and object are separable: the concept admits of being "manipulated" apart from the object. And all mental life in a certain sense just amounts to the attempt to get concept and object to coincide—an attempt that eternally fails, because eternally losing itself in unending series. One thing only in all the world is so constituted that in regard to it no separation of concept and object is found—I myself! For that which I conceive myself as, that even I myself am; and every attempt to form a concept is just a form of myself. Here the concept of myself is experience, actuality itself. I myself am the unique, to me accessible, pure actuality of the world. *Buddhism is the teaching of actuality.* It starts out with the only pure actuality of the world, and from this point proceeds to suck the entire play of world-events without exception into the whirlpool of its thinking. And with this we find ourselves in the presence of the Buddha-thought itself.

V

THE DOCTRINE OF THE BUDDHA

I BEGIN with the question that concludes the third essay: "How can it be possible for faith and science to possess opposed conceptions when both actually start out from one and the same given thing, the world?"

All that exists presents itself on one hand as "something that is," and on the other as "something that happens"—that is to say, as something found in a state of perpetual change, as processes.

Where something happens, there adequate causes must be present. These adequate causes must be forces.

All processes—*i.e.* the entire play of world-events—fall into two great classes: those *that are maintained*, dead processes, and those *that maintain themselves*, living processes; the latter presenting themselves, on the one hand, as processes of combustion, as flame, and on the other as processes of alimentation, as living beings.

All dead processes can be interpreted or read as falls. Their type is the falling stone. A stone does not fall because of an indwelling force that causes its falling; it only falls because it has previously been raised, because between it and the surface of the earth there exists a difference of tension. Its fall thus signifies that force must have been present, in the sense that it must *previously* have been active; for otherwise the difference in position of stone and surface of the earth could never have come about. When physics interprets the fall of the stone in differing fashion—namely, by having it caused by the attractive force of the earth's surface in action during the fall—this is purely a working hypothesis, advanced solely in the interest of a uniform physical world-theory.

To much the same effect as the falling stone, every physical happening without exception is to be interpreted or read, whether it concern mechanical, chemical, thermal, electrical, magnetic, or any other such-like phenomena. All alike are to be taken as falls from places of higher to places of lower tension. The import of each and all is only that forces, actuating impulsions, *must once have been present.* In each case we really have to do not with actions but with reactions.

The proof that no actual forces are here at work is to be found in the fact that the process ceases so soon as the differences of tension are adjusted.

This world of reactions is the given province of all science.

Science, because bent upon furnishing demonstration, has a title to existence only where there is nothing that is not perceptible to sense. Where there are actual living processes, there *actual forces must be present.* A force, however, can never be perceptible to sense; for everything perceptible to sense necessitates the question as to its adequate cause—that is, as to the force in virtue of which it exists. Where there are dead, re-actual processes, there forces are not in action themselves, and hence force is not a real but only a conceptual necessity, a mere logical presumption. Hence also in the interpretation of this re-actual world, it is always possible to slur over, to eliminate the question as to actual forces, and to replace these latter by the various differences of tension, of potentiality, and thus remain wholly within the domain of the sensible.

Such a position is quite permissible to a science that devotes itself exclusively to technique, *i.e.* aims at nothing more than to measure and calculate in advance, for it is only re actual proceedings that admit of being measured and calculated in advance. When such and such a planet will occupy such and such a position in the heavens, this admits of being calculated beforehand with the most perfect accuracy. But whether this next moment I shall twirl my thumb to the right or to the left, that no science, no academy in the world can compute in advance.

The position which science takes up towards the world—a rejection in principle of all that is not perceptible to sense—of necessity involves restriction to the re-actual world, and therewith the mechanical conception of the play of world-events.

Yet once more. This conception is perfectly legitimate so long as it confines itself to the re-actual world. But it becomes an anomaly the moment it seeks to pass beyond this re-actual world —the moment a man tries to read the actual world, the living processes, according to the same scheme —that of a falling. For here it is actual forces that are at work; here the question as to actual forces declines to be eliminated or exempted by acts of intellectual violence that by their repugnancy to common sense bring about their own downfall. Later on we shall have to revert to these attempts to interpret physically living beings, the entire man as a falling, a mere process of adjustment, and to explain consciousness in purely mechanical fashion. Though one should be able to "read" the animal organism after physical formulas in never so far-reaching a manner, though one should be able to co-ordinate the whole process of alimentation, the housekeeping of life, in never so perfect a fashion with the law of the conservation of energy, nothing has been gained withal that might settle the question as to what exactly that is which keeps this mechanism going: such a question is never once touched on at all; nay, by this method of procedure it is deliberately pushed on one side, as much and as long as ever is possible, until straightforward, natural thinking rises in revolt against such behaviour as a learned pastime and demands actuality.

Hence:—

That particular form of mental life which rejects in principle what is not perceptible to sense, thereby of necessity is confined to the re-actual world. If it seeks to encroach upon actual processes, it must arbitrarily leave out of consideration that in them which is *essential*, the forces at work in them,—whereby it falls into absurdities that speedily take their revenge by raising problems that are insoluble.

This form of mental life is universally called "*science*," whereby, it must be admitted, the more or less active counter-currents—those of the teleological conception of things—are passed over unnoticed. Science, properly speaking, is always *materialistic*, and its conception of the play of world-events always strictly *mechanical*. For it the adequate cause of each occurrence is simply another occurrence. Adequate causes remain perceptible to sense.

Opposite to it stands faith.

Faith is that particular form of mental life which recognizes an "imperceptible to sense in itself," *i.e. believes*, and so doing, assumes a universal "adequate cause in itself" for the entire play of world-events. From this it follows that the living processes are the true province of all faith. In them alone are actual forces, *i.e.* that which is imperceptible to sense, actively at work.

As soon as faith seeks to make use of its intuition, *i.e.* seeks to supply a world-view, it finds itself in the same predicament as science. Just as this latter, as world-theory, is obliged to read the actual processes according to the scheme of the re-actual, so faith as world-theory is obliged to read the re-actual processes according to the scheme of the actual; in other words, it must represent the world, even to the extent that it represents itself as purely a falling, as guided by a divine force. Here not a hair can drop from my head, not a stone fall to the ground, without a divine decree having taken an active part therein as adequate cause, an idea which, thought out, leads to the absurdity of the doctrine of predestination, with which doctrine faith robs herself of the possibility of her own existence. For, where there is predestination, there is no free will; where there is no free will there is no soul; and where there is no soul there is no God.

That which, in being thought out, deprives itself of the possibility of existence is contrary to sense, and as such, a nescience, like illusion and error.

Between and raised above both these opposed positions stands the Buddha.

This is his teaching:—

All that is, all processes whatsoever, whether they be re-actual or whether they be actual, all is Sankhāra. This is the epistemological key-word of Buddhism. Its meaning is, All is of a compounded, of a conditioned nature. The Buddha concurs with modern science in so far as it rejects an uncompounded, an unconditioned, a unity in itself, a soul-substance, or whatever else one chooses to style it. As already shown, for science one event is entirely conditioned by other events; she makes the adequate cause of one phenomenon of life simply other phenomena of life, and thereby frankly remains always in the realm of the sensible, the demonstrable — thereby limits herself, however, to the re-actual side of the world. Among the actual, self-sustaining processes, this position has no foothold whatever; for in these actual forces *must* be present, and as such never by any means can be perceptible to sense, thus also can never be the subject of science.

One can only speak of an actual view of the world where the *actual* world is concerned. I comprehend it when I discern the adequate causes of the actual processes, that is, the forces actively at work in them.

Now the word *Sankhāra* signifies not only "the

compounded," "the conditioned," but also "the compounding," "the conditioning," somewhat the same as the German word *Wirkung* may equally well be held to signify the result effected by the cause as the actual effecting of that result itself. In the former case it signifies that forces have been present; it has reference to the re-actual world. In the latter case it means that forces *are* present; it refers to the actual world. Like the word *Wirkung*, the word *Sankhāra* embraces both these aspects.

With reference to the self-sustaining, actual processes, the teaching of the Buddha proceeds:—

All living beings exist by reason of forces. Accordingly the Buddha here agrees with faith, inasmuch as he recognizes the presence in living beings of what is imperceptible to sense; for a force can never be perceptible to sense.

But whilst faith makes every living being exist in virtue of a universal force, and thereby assumes an "adequate cause in itself"—as a transcendent, an absolute, a god—which means "believing," thus landing itself in the predicament of having to interpret the re-actual side of the world also by this "force"; the Buddha on his part teaches:—

Every living being is here in virtue of individual force peculiar to him alone. This force hereby in quite a literal sense becomes an *in-force*, an *en-ergy*. The Buddha teaches the existence of *actual energies*, in contradistinction to faith's universal force.

This *in-force* peculiar to every living being, and thereby *unique*, is called by the Buddha *the Kamma* (Sanskrit, Karma) of such a living being.

Kamma means nothing but "*the working*."

Kamma is that in virtue of which a living being manifests activity after its own unique fashion—in its own unique way reacts upon the external world; it is that which makes a living being to be an individuality, a personality.

Every living being is a thing unique, and as such incapable of being compared, incapable of being repeated, as re-actual processes are not, since in them no actual forces are active. Though I see, hear, smell, taste, touch, and think the same thing, it is yet my own, a something unique that I see, hear, smell, taste, touch, and think.

I am a thing unique, a personality in virtue of my *in-force*, of my Kamma.

The distinction between an *in-force* and a universal force is this:—

The latter is a something existing of itself, a something existing of its own authority, *i.e.* a creation of faith; *whilst an in-force has being solely in dependence upon its material*, only with the help of the material worked up by it. As "heat," "light," "electricity," and so forth, are words of no meaning in the absence of a material in which to manifest themselves, so *in-force* Kamma, is a word of no meaning in the absence of its material.

This material of Kamma is by the Buddha called the *Khandhas.*

They are five in number, these namely:—

Corporeality, Sensation, Perception, Discriminations, and Consciousness.

The word Khandha may be variously translated as group, aggregation, coagulation, formation.

The Khandhas do not represent *parts, pieces* of the *I*-process, but *phases, forms of development*, something like the shape, colour and odour in a flower. An actual process, a proceeding of the nature of combustion or alimentation, never can have any parts. It is only in connection with dead products like a table, a chair, and so forth, that one can speak of such; as also where one intentionally conceives of things after this fashion with a definite end in view. From the purely anatomical standpoint, the eye, the brain, the lungs, the liver, and so forth in a corpse, are parts of the body. Truly speaking, in the living person they are forms of development, since all have come forth from one common root. One must keep firm hold of this if one makes claim to think in terms of *actuality*.

"*Material*," in contradistinction to matter, is that which is specially worked up by an energy. "Matter in itself" is all as hollow a figment of thought, projecting like a blind end out of actuality, as is "force in itself." Both are products of faith: the one pertaining to science, the other to religions. *Actuality has no "substance," no "matter," but only material, i.e.* matter worked up by energies; it has no "force," but only energies, *i.e.* forces apparelled, substantialized, so to speak. Actuality always and everywhere is only the unity of opposites—a process.

To allow one's thought to occupy itself with a "force by itself," or a "substance by itself," means to work with half actualities possessing as much content of actuality as one side of a sheet of paper imagined by itself. I assert that to think thus is an intellectual *breach of discipline*.

Now the manner in which I represent myself corporeally, receive sensations, acquire perceptions, exercise discriminations, become conscious of things, is one peculiar to me and to me alone, a thing unique. This means:—

In every motion, corporeal as mental, physical as psychical, I am the form of Kamma itself.

This fact, that every living being is wholly and entirely the embodiment of his Kamma, is expressed by the Buddha in the word "anattā," not-self. All beings are "anattā," but this does not in any way mean, as science would fain make out, that they are all of a purely re-actual nature. It only means that they do not conceal within them a "force in itself," a "constant in itself," but are *out and out processes of combustion, of alimentation,* such as cannot conceal any "constant in itself," since at every moment of their existence they represent a fresh biological value, and hence hold nothing that could possibly justify the notion of an *I*-identity, a genuine self.

"The body, O monks, is 'anattā.' If the body were the self (*attā*), then this corporeal frame could not go to decay, and in this corporeal frame, this wish of mine would find fulfilment: 'Let my corporeal part be thus! Let not my corporeal part be so!' But, O monks, because the corporeal is anattā, therefore does the corporeal go to decay, and the wish, 'Let my corporeal part be thus! Let not my corporeal part be so!' does not find fulfilment."[1]

Following the like scheme, the remaining four Khandhas are then dealt with; and so, step by step, the idea of an *I*-identity is banished.

The Buddha conceives of the entire *actual* world, *i.e.* the world of self-sustaining processes as an

[1] *Mahāvagga*, i. 6, and many other passages.

infinitely large number of combustion processes. Every being burns in virtue of a purely individual *in-force*, Kamma.

This his world-conception is given by the Buddha in that famous "Fire Sermon" which, shortly after the inauguration of his career of activity as a teacher, he delivered to his followers on a hill in the neighbourhood of Gayā. It is the "Sermon on the Mount" of Buddhism.

"All things, O monks, is a burning. And why, O monks, is all a burning? The eye, O monks, is a burning. Visual consciousness [that is, the conscious representation that results in virtue of visual impressions] is a burning. Visual contact [*i.e.* the act of the encountering of eye and objects] is a burning. That which arises in virtue of visual contact, be it a pleasant, be it an unpleasant sensation, be it a neither pleasant nor unpleasant sensation, is a burning."[1]

Following the like scheme, the ear and the audible, the nose and the olfactory, the tongue and the gustatory, the body and the tangible, thought and concepts are then dealt with.

The place of the Buddha between and above the opposites, faith and science, may be briefly formulated as follows:—

Faith says, "*Everything stands*,"—namely, in the place in which it has been set by that "force in itself," God. Science says, "*Everything falls*," which means that she neglects actual forces in general. The *Buddha* says, "*Everything burns*," meaning that every process exists in virtue of a single *in-force*, peculiar to itself.

[1] *Mahāvagga*, i. 21.

And now as a consequence there follows this question :—

" If through and through, without residue, I am a form of Kamma, where is to be found the position from which I can comprehend myself *as such* ? " For every position, without exception, of sheer necessity must itself again be a form of Kamma.

Kamma, the *in-force*, is that which gives to the process concerned, to the living being, *foothold, coherence, continuity*.

As such it presents itself to me the individual *immediately as consciousness*. In consciousness I comprehend myself as a something existing in virtue of an *in-force*, inasmuch as consciousness on one hand is that which gives continuity to the *I*-process; on the other hand, however, at every moment presents a fresh biological, Kammic value, even as cannot be otherwise in any combustion process.

Be it well noted, however, Consciousness is not the Kamma. That would give us Kamma as an identity. But Kamma in the course of its self-acting development *becomes* consciousness. Consciousness is the *ultimate value* (*Grenzwert*), in which at every moment of its existence the form of the energy and the energy itself merge and mingle, and consequently that which gives to the *I*-process not only *conceptual*, but also *actual* continuity.

Faith adopts as adequate cause a transcendent force, an imperceptible to sense in itself. Science rejects all that is imperceptible to sense and adopts as the adequate cause of one occurrence other occurrences. The Buddha teaches that the actual processes have being in virtue of an *in-force*, *i.e.* an imperceptible to sense; but this imperceptible to sense is so, *not* "*in itself*," as a transcendent in itself, but in the course of its automatic development, *for the individual becomes perceptible to sense as consciousness.*

It is in this sense that we are to understand the matter when the Buddha, having specified consciousness as one of the five Khandhas, thus making it a *form* of Kamma, upon another occasion says, "*It is Cetana* (*thinking*) *that I call Kamma.*" In a Burmese school I once listened to the following questions and answers: *Teacher*, "What is Kamma?" *Pupil*, "Cetana." *Teacher*, "What is Cetana?" *Pupil*, "Kamma."

In this sense is to be understood the frequently recurring formula: "In dependence upon individuality (*nāma-rūpa*) arises consciousness (*viññāna*); in dependence upon consciousness arises individuality." For *in-force*, in contradistinction to a transcendent universal force, is something that only exists in dependence upon its material.

The understanding of this point will be rendered much easier by a comparison with a flame.

In a flame each moment of its existence represents a specific degree of heat which, as such, *is the power* to set up a succeeding moment of ignition. This power is actualized wherever and for as long as inflammable matter, fuel, is present. The inflammable matter, so to say, is the liberating provocation that causes this power, this potential energy which the flame every moment represents in virtue of its heat to enter into life, and shows it the way into living energy.

But with this conversion into living energy, *i.e.*

with the fact that a new ignition moment is called into life, a new degree of heat, a new value in potential energy also is produced, which, as the succeeding ignition moment, anew passes over into living energy, thus forming a repetition of the whole proceeding. It is a process which may be briefly designated as a self-charging. The self-discharging, the act of the passage of potential into living energy, is simultaneously the charging anew with potential energy. Precisely in this consists the nature of the self-active. The self-active is that which possesses the faculty, the power to sustain itself; and this self-sustaining, when analyzed, exhibits itself in the form of self-charging. If potential energy has passed over into living energy, there is here no need of an accession of foreign energy to fashion a new store of potential energy. This new store is implied in the discharge itself. Energy, actual energy, is not something that must receive an impetus from without in order to come into activity, it is activity, action itself, and proves itself such by itself; and all that is necessary is to comprehend, to comprise it in this its characteristic quality.

That this perfectly natural conception to us has become so unnatural, must be laid to the charge of our habits of thought, trained one-sidedly as we have been, along the lines of mechanical views. Where something happens, we look for some impulse from without; but we ought never to forget that science does not give the actual world at all, but only a re-actual world; in which world, to be sure, impulses must be given if anything is to happen at all. The mechanical world-theory is simply a "reading" of the play of world-events in order to give computation and determination in advance; never under any circumstances does it furnish an insight into actuality itself. Actuality is action out of itself; it is the self-active. And all the insoluble problems in which science loses her way when she seeks to carry the mechanical comprehension of the play of world-events from the reversible processes where it is possible and legitimate, over to the non-reversible processes, all in the last analysis amount to this, that one is trying to demonstrate something—*i.e.* the biological process—from external preconditions, which along such lines can never be demonstrated, not because in itself incapable of demonstration, but because it is demonstrating itself through itself.

This the genuine thinker must absolutely hold to. Actuality is action itself, not something that first must be acted upon. Everything re-actual is thinkable only as the sequel of a push requires a push for its explanation. Everything that is actual burns.

After this, what takes place in the *I*-process becomes comprehensible.

Here the passing over from potential to living energy has its counterpart in the *volitional movements*. At every moment of its existence the *I*-process represents a specific value in potential energy which there where the external world enters with its "liberating" provocations, ever and again passes over into living energy as volitional movement. Every discharge in the form of a volitional movement is a charging afresh with potential energy. It is a self-sustaining proceeding in the fullest sense of the words. The volitional movements are the ever repeated new foothold which the *I* fashions for itself, the ever repeated "sustenance" wherewith it provides itself afresh.

The all-important point about this conception is that one should clearly see that Kamma *does not, like a cord of some sort of solid material*, thread itself through the *I*-process, as would be bound to be the case with an *I*-force, whether dubbed soul, or life-force, or whatever else; but that in every volitional movement it ever and again springs up anew out of a material to which it itself, in the first place, ever and again lends the power to this end. The material has to be *Kammatized* so as to be able to give Kamma the opportunity to spring up anew. As in the friction of one piece of wood with another, heat springs up, and ever and again springs up with each repetition of the friction, so in the friction of the *I*-process with the external world, with things, ever and again new volitional movements spring up. "Somewhat, O monk, as when two pieces of wood are laid one upon the other, are rubbed one against the other, heat arises, fire springs up; and when these two pieces of wood are parted, are separated, the heat that has arisen, disappears, ceases; even so, O monk, by reason of a contact of a pleasurable nature, a pleasurable sensation springs up."[1]

This the reply, the reaction peculiar to itself of the *I*-process to the external world, a reply, a reaction that takes the form of volitional movements, this is Kamma, the action of this *I*-process. That which as regards all the rest of the world is imperceptible

[1] *Majjhima Nikāya*, Sutta 140.

to sense, here in the self-acting, the spontaneous development of the individual, *becomes* perceptible to sense. Nothing else whatever is concealed within the *I*-process: itself has disclosed itself. As in a flame there is nothing hidden and concealed, its activity constituting its entire being, so in the *I*-process there is nothing hidden and concealed. Its activity constitutes its entire being, and this activity *in full entirety* is disclosed in consciousness to the individual himself, and to him only. And nothing more is needed than to comprehend actuality simply as that which it is.

This insight into the *I* as a pure combustion process places the whole problem of existence upon an entirely new foundation.

In a combustion process every moment of its existence is a *setting-up-of-life* just as much as an *entering-into-life*. The *I*-process in all its activities, whether of the corporeal or of the mental variety, is a constant growing up of life itself, an arising, a perpetual refashioning, setting up anew, inasmuch as the energy perpetually works up, assimilates fresh material. Here is no *I* that experiences; no *I* that thinks, speaks, does. I do not *have* all this as my functions, but this doing, speaking, thinking—this itself I *am*. In all this I ever and again am being built anew, just as in the assimilating of the nourishment of which I partake, I ever and again am built anew,—it is all the one same process of combustion, differing only in the surrounding circumstances and antecedent conditions.

"What, O monks, is the arising of the world? By reason of the eye and of forms there arises visual consciousness. The conjunction of the three constitutes contact. In dependence upon contact arises sensation. In dependence upon sensation arises the thirst for life. In dependence upon the thirst for life arises clinging. In dependence upon clinging arises becoming. In dependence upon becoming arises birth (as the birth of a fresh biological impulsion). In dependence upon birth arises old age and death."

This passage recurs with great frequency in the Scriptures. Following the same scheme there are next dealt with—hearing and sounds, smell and odours, taste and flavours, the body and contacts, thinking and concepts.

In every one of its activities, at every moment of its existence, the *I*-process is not something that possesses arising as a function, but it *is* the arising itself, as the flame *is* the arising itself. And it *is* the arising itself because it burns, because it exists in virtue of an individual energy. It is the thirst for life, the impulsion towards life, which *upholds life*, causes it ever and again to spring up anew, and *is life itself*; in exactly the same way that the heat of a flame upholds the flame and is the flame itself. We do not *have* the impulse to life—that calls for a *conscious* impulse—but we *are* the life-impulse itself.

A lay adherent upon one occasion inquires of the nun Dhammadinna :—

" Personality, personality, they say, O venerable One. But what does the Exalted One say is the personality ? "

To which the nun replies :—

" The five forms of clinging (*upādānakkhandhā*) is the personality, the Exalted One has said ; these namely: the form of clinging that refers to body, the form of clinging that refers to sensation, the form of clinging that refers to perception, the form of clinging that refers to discriminations, the form of clinging that refers to consciousness. . . ."

"The arising of personality, the arising of personality, they say, O venerable One. But what, O venerable One, does the Exalted One say is the arising of personality?"

"This thirst for life (*tanhā*) that leads to re-birth, bound up with lust and craving, now here, now there, revelling in delight—namely, the impulse towards sensuality, the impulse towards existence, the impulse towards present well-being (without regard to any possible future). This, friend, so the Exalted One has said, is the arising of personality."[1]

The distinction between faith and science on the one hand and the Buddha on the other, may be formulated thus:—

According to faith, living beings all possess as adequate cause for their existence a transcendent force, usually called "soul." According to science, living beings as well as all re-actual processes, have their adequate cause entirely in what is perceptible to sense; which means that science derives living beings simply and solely from their begetters—mother and father—thus entangling herself in her insoluble problem of heredity. The Buddha on his part teaches *that every being is adequate cause to itself*. As a flame maintains itself by its own heat, so every *I*-process maintains itself by its volitional movements.

Now it is an incontestable biological fact that

[1] *Majjhima Nikāya*, Sutta 44.

man, and along with him a considerable proportion of the animal world, originate in the union of a maternal ovum-cell with a paternal sperm-cell. How can the teaching of the Buddha that beings are their own adequate causes be brought into line with this fact?

It is just here that the Buddha breaks with vulgar thinking in a manner that at first sight seems out of all reason.

He teaches that that which mother and father furnish in the act of union is only, so to speak, the material of the new living being, only represents the *possibility* of a new individuality; that this material is developed into an individuality only through the advent of an individual energy. "By the conjunction of three things, O monks, does the formation of a germ of life come about. If mother and father come together, but it is not the mother's proper period, and the exciting impulse does not present itself, a germ of life is not planted. If mother and father come together and it is the mother's proper period, but the exciting impulse does not present itself, a germ of life is not planted. If, however, O monks, mother and father come together and it is the mother's proper period, and the exciting impulse presents itself, then a germ of life is there planted."[1]

As the igniting spark catches, breaks in, and, taking the kindling wood and the oxygen of the atmosphere which, but for its advent, would have lain beside one another for long enough without any reaction, fuses them together into the individuality, "flame," so does the individual energy joining

[1] *Majjhima Nikāya*, Sutta 38.

up with the material of procreation, fuse ovum- and sperm-cell together into the new personality.

This "in-breaking" energy that joins up with the raw material of procreation,—this is the Kamma of some other existence which has been unable any longer to maintain its form against the pressure of the external world, an occurrence which we usually denominate "death." The Kamma of the disintegrating existence—so the Buddha teaches—at the moment of death passes over into a new abode, plants itself, breaks in here in new inflammable material, kindles a new *I*-process, fashions a new *I*-sayer. And as the igniting spark *becomes* the flame by developing itself, growing, unfolding along with the material of which it has taken hold, so does Kamma *become* the new form of existence by developing itself, growing, unfolding along with the material of which it has taken hold. In other words, *I am the form of my Kamma. I am my Kamma corporealised.*

This Kamma series it is which constitutes the *actual* genealogical tree of a living being. As the genealogical tree of a fire does not lead in the direction of the forest or the coal-mine whence its material was derived, but back to the flame from out of which the kindling spark took hold, so the genealogical tree of living beings does not run back in the direction of progenitors but in the direction of the Kamma, the direction of a disintegrating existence. "Heirs of deeds," therefore, the Buddha calls living beings, not heirs of mother and father; and, "springing from the womb of Kamma (*kammayonī*)." The Kamma, in virtue of which I now say "*I*," derives from a previous existence; the "*I*-

sayer" of this previous existence, on his part again, derives from a previous existence, and so on further and further back in a series that never has had a beginning. *At every moment of my existence I am the final member of a beginningless series of "I-sayers."* The Kamma at this moment active in me —it has never not existed, never not been active. This is what means a self-sustaining process. Such a process can never have had a beginning; for then it would be no self-sustaining thing, it would have been created, either by a god, or by external circumstances and antecedent conditions. It would be no actual process but a product. As soon as clear cognition brings me the insight that I am a pure process of combustion, *i.e.* sustain myself, along with that insight is given as a logical necessity beginninglessness.

Individual beginninglessness is the key-word, the guiding clue to the Buddha-thought. In it is exhausted the teaching of Kamma. The *I*-process has its *in-force*, its Kamma from out a previous existence. Otherwise expressed: The *I*-process is not the result of an impact, has not been set going, but burns on from beginninglessness down to this present moment, itself ever and again *perpetuating itself.* Whenever an existence disintegrates, the Kamma in virtue of which it has been burning takes hold anew in a new location and there sets alight a new *I*-process that unfolds itself into a new personality. *The Buddha teaches re-births.*

The self-perpetuation of the individual energies, the Kammas, in the formation of ever new individualities, is by the Buddha called "Samsāra."

This word is most frequently translated, "the

circling round of re-births,"—a rendering that may easily lead to a false conception. Where the entire universe is nothing but a huge summation of single combustion processes, there no circling round can be; there each moment of existence always and everywhere is something that never before has been and never again will be. With the translation "circling round of re-births," one only works with physics and its reversible processes; one is in danger of apprehending life mechanically. As a matter of fact, "Samsāra" means nothing but the "together-wandering," the ascent and descent of the beings in the universe, that ever and again, now here now there, come into manifestation anew, according as their Kamma here or there takes hold.

"Without beginning, without end is this Samsāra. A beginning of beings encompassed by nescience who, fettered by the thirst for life, pass on to ever new births, verily is not to be perceived."

The thinking man naturally asks, "Is there any proof of such a teaching? or must it simply be believed?" In the latter case it were as worthless to the genuine thinker as is every religion of faith. Whether I call that on which I believe, force or energy, god or Kamma, makes no essential difference.

But to this question there are two answers—an answer of a real, and an answer of an abstract nature.

The answer of real nature is supplied by the Buddha when he affirms of himself that simultaneously with the attainment of his Buddha-knowledge, he acquired the faculty of remembering his previous forms of existence back into eras of time the most stupendously remote. He teaches, however, that every one who, like himself, has wrestled his way to the same knowledge, obtains this same capacity of calling to remembrance his previous states of existence.

Now the Buddha-knowledge is no supernatural illumination, but consists simply of a clear insight into the nature of my own existence—or rather, in the removal of a false conception as to myself, the conception of the "*I*" as an identity. To attain to this insight, all that is needed is reflection and instruction. This seemingly supernatural character of the faculty of remembering previous existences is thus "supernatural" only in the sense that the telephone or the Röntgen ray or wireless telegraphy is supernatural to untutored savages. We are merely lacking in the prerequisite conditions as respects cognition, and in the intellectual technique.

This much safely may be said, that the biological possibility of memory of the distant past can only be brought to bear upon the several existences in so far as these themselves have run their course in touch with the power of memory, in touch with consciousness. To try to make this faculty extend over the embryonal periods also, would be absurd, since here the organic possibilities of such memory—the sense-organs, namely—are not developed, and so there is nothing there for one to remember. Hence, when he speaks of his previous existences the Buddha says, not, "I remember having left such and such a womb," but, "I remember having been of such a name, such a family, such a rank, such a calling; having experienced such and such weal and woe, and such a departure from life." Here what is meant by the constantly recurring phrase "*evam āyupariyanto*"—"thus was the term, the end of my life"—is not physical death, but the ending of that section of the individuality which runs its course self-illuminated, under the designation of consciousness. This end may indeed synchronize with the physical end, death, but it may also precede it by a longer or shorter period of time.

In corresponding terms the Buddha goes on to say, "Departing thence, elsewhere I appeared anew. There now I was, bore such a name," and so on. The memories of the past adhere only to those phases of existence that are illumined by consciousness.

It may be asked, "By what means is it possible to acquire such a faculty of remembering the distant past?"

I reply, "I do not know." I can only suggest an analogy. One must extinguish one's own light in order to see the light that shines through the chink in a neighbouring room. In somewhat the same fashion, a man must have extinguished his own light—the notion of an *I*-identity—and won to the Buddha-knowledge, in order to see himself emerge recurrently as a something luminous in consciousness further and yet further away in the "dark backward and abysm of time,"—one lucent phase, ever and again revealing itself, anterior to the other, until the last faint glimmer is lost in the dim dusk teeming with life, of the beginningless infinitudes.

The Buddha himself instances a definite limit to the capacity to recall to memory past existences, up to which limit he himself attained. Here we have the best possible proof that we have to do, not with a supernatural enlightenment, a species of omniscience, but simply with an intellectual technique which as being purely intellectual, presupposes a certain grade of cognition. If we may put any confidence in the texts, there were in the days of the Buddha, and in those days of which the "Chants of the monks and nuns" tell us, quite a large number of persons who had acquired this faculty. If some one here interjects, "Such a thing is impossible!" he resembles a man at the foot of a hill to whom another standing on the top has described what he sees from that point of vantage, and who retorts, "It is quite impossible that you should see all this. I have eyes in my head as well as you. I look upon the same world as you do and I perceive nothing whatever of all this. Consequently your imagination must be playing tricks with you."

So much for the real answer. The abstract answer presents itself in the light of an intellectual necessity.

Kamma is that which gives continuity to the *I*-process. As such it presents itself to me the individual immediately as consciousness. Consciousness, rightly comprehended, tells me that the *I*-process gives to itself its own coherence; which means that it is self-acting; which in turn means that it is beginningless. I experience the self-perpetuation, the burning of the *I*-process in consciousness. But just as Kamma conducts from one moment of existence to the next, so does it conduct from one existence to the next.

Should one wish to render this procedure in comprehensible language, one can come at it no otherwise than simply by saying, "Consciousness passes over from existence to existence." "Kamma" in itself conveys no more meaning than, for example, the word *I*, which indicates anybody and everybody without distinction, and only acquires *actual* significance with reference to myself. In exactly the same way "Kamma," the force in virtue of which every single living creature has being, acquires *actual* significance only as my own consciousness. Kamma *as such* has being only as consciousness.

It is in this sense that those passages are to be understood, so obscure to our scholars, in which the Buddha speaks of *viññāṇa* (consciousness) as that which plants itself in the new womb. Addressing his disciple Ānanda, he says, "If, Ānanda, consciousness did not pass into the womb, would it then be possible for the (new) individuality to differentiate itself?"[1]

Among the Theras of Ceylon the established expression for the Kamma that passes over from one existence to the next is *paṭisandhiviññāṇa*, a word which means "the again-linking-up consciousness," the consciousness that ever and again supplies the bond between existence and existence.

That there is here no thought of consciousness as "something in itself," as soul, as an identity, is made abundantly clear in the following passage:—

A monk named Sati, as the outcome of his own cogitations, arrives at the conclusion that "consciousness" is something that in the progress of re-births

[1] "Differentiate itself" is meant to equate *samucchissatha*, a word for which it is difficult to find an adequate equivalent. It signifies the self-integration of the new being simultaneously with its severance from the maternal organism.

passes over as *anaññaŋ*, as "not-other"—that is, as an identity, as a spiritual substance. He is reprimanded by the Buddha in these words: "Have not I in many and diverse ways expounded consciousness as something arising always in dependence upon somewhat? Without adequate cause there is no coming to be of consciousness."[1]

To much the same effect runs a passage in the *Visuddhi Magga*:—

"But it is to be understood that this latter consciousness (that of the new existence is meant) did not come to the present existence from the previous one, and also that it is only to causes contained in the old existence that its present appearance is due."[2]

Only when one understands that *Viññāṇa* (consciousness) is Kamma itself, does a "consciousness" that passes over from existence to existence become divested of its seeming senselessness.

When, for example, I say, "The American heat-wave has passed over to Europe," this does not mean that an absolutely definite something called "heat-wave" has set out on a journey. It only means that certain pulses of energy which manifest themselves to sense under the form of a wave of heat are making their presence known in a new locality. In just the same way, when I say, "Consciousness passes over from one existence to another," this does not mean that an absolutely definite something called "consciousness" goes forth upon its travels, but that the pulse of energy of the *I*-process which, wherever it is present at all

[1] *Majjhima Nikāya*, Sutta 38.
[2] *Buddhism in Translations*, by H. C. Warren, p. 239.

as such manifests itself as consciousness, makes its presence known in a new location. Should any one insist upon conceiving of the heat-wave as a something travelling, he would rightly become the butt of ridicule. In similar wise, the scholars of the west with their profound researches into this "consciousness" that passes over from existence to existence, make fair marks for jest and laughter. Here, of course, they are only working further along in the tracks of physiology and biology, both of which so long as they seek for a "seat" of consciousness, labour under a like tragi-comic misconception.

No good purpose is to be served by instancing here in detail all the crass misconceptions of which our western scholars are guilty in the interpretation of this point. That would only be to burden this book on its way with quite unnecessary ballast. Wherever the reader meets with such misconceptions, he can correct them for himself on the lines of the foregoing explanations. In passing, however, it may be mentioned that he will meet with such misconceptions in pretty nearly every book about Buddhism.

And now we stand confronted by the question :—

"After what fashion is one to picture to oneself the passing over of Kamma from one existence to another?"

To us in the West who have been reared in the mechanistic views of science and admit of the inductive method alone in argument, this seems the point most obscure among all the obscurities we find in the Buddha-thought. In the Buddha's days, however, this point seems to have been so completely free from anything savouring of the problematical that the Buddha himself would seem never to have found it necessary to express himself categorically upon it.

If to-day one asks the Theras in Ceylon or Burma how one ought to think of this passing over, one receives the unfailing reply, "It is not the case that 'something' passes over."

Here one must fall back upon the works of the commentators for fuller information.

In the *Milinda Pañha* (the *Questions of King Milinda*), a work that in Ceylon is held in the highest esteem, there occurs the following passage:—

(The King says): "Bhante (Reverend Sir) Nagasena, does the connection (with the next existence) take place without anything passing over?" (The Monk Nagasena replies): "Yes, great King, the connection takes place without anything passing over." "Give me an example of connection taking place without anything passing over!" "Suppose a man to light one lamp at another, does one light here pass over to the other?" "No, bhante." "In just the same way the connection takes place without anything passing over."[1]

Hereupon the question arises:—

"This previous existence of which I am the immediate continuation—am I this itself or am I another?"

A further passage in the same book, the *Milinda Pañha*, runs:—

"He who is born—is he the same or is he another?" "Neither the same, neither another."

[1] *Pāli Text*, P.T.S. edition, p. 71.

"Give me an illustration!" "Suppose a man to light a lamp: would it burn the whole night through?" "Yes, it would burn the whole night through." "Now, is the flame of the first watch the same with the flame of the middle watch?" "No, indeed!" "Or is the flame of the middle watch the same with the flame of the last watch?" "No, indeed!" "Then is the lamp of the first watch one, the lamp of the middle watch another, and the lamp of the last watch yet another?" "No, indeed! In dependence upon one and the same (lamp) the light burns all the night through." "Even so does the continuity of men and things come about. One arises, another passes away. On the instant, as it were, without before or after, the linking up is effected. Thus it is not oneself, nor yet is it another, that passes on (and constitutes) each last present phase of consciousness."

With this we arrive at the crucial point. *The passing over ensues on the instant, immediately, not in space and time.*

Buddhism, if it is to satisfy the thinker, here will have to come to an understanding with modern physics. In a succeeding essay this will be attempted. For the present, as preliminary, we hold fast only to the fact.

The *I*-process as being the form of an *in-force*, at every moment of its existence represents a certain value in potential energy, a certain unique state of tension, an individual tendency. This tendency it is which at the breaking up of the old form immediately establishes itself in the new location.

But where? Is this new location always ready waiting to take up the new Kamma?

A universe that consists of nothing but a huge summation of combustion processes, finds itself, so to speak, in a perpetual *status nascens*. Here every fresh moment represents a new, unique, biological, Kammic value, which as such never before has been and never again will be.

Now all actual happenings come to pass in virtue of peculiar attunements—in the language of chemistry, specific affinities. A body, a process, acts upon another because in virtue of its peculiar attunement it can and must act on that other. But where the entire universe is a something existing in a perpetual *status nascens*, there is, strictly speaking, no such thing as a *being attuned*, but only an *each-after-other self-attuning*, taking place anew with each new moment. The entire actual happenings of a world from this point of view become something that does not *have laws*, but *is law itself*; a thought as sublime as it is terrible. The significance of Buddhism for a morality is completely dominated by it.

Hence, where the actual play of world-events alone is in question, the same is indicated by the word "Dhamma" (law or norm). All beings, even as they are Sankhāra, are also Dhamma.[1] Kamma,

[1] These two words are not, as most western scholars aver, altogether synonymous, for "Dhamma" embraces everything—actual as well as re-actual processes. When, on the other hand, it is desired particularly to specify the re-actual processes, the word "Sañkhāra" serves the purpose. The stereotyped formula: "All Sankhāras are transient; all Sankhāras are painful; all *Dhammas* are non-self," is not based upon any caprice nor yet upon metrical considerations (as Oldenburg asserts in his *Buddha*, 1897 edition, p. 291), for the prose versions render the three phrases in exactly the same form, as may be seen by a reference to the *Majjhima Nikāya*, Sutta 35. On the contrary, the formula is founded upon a clearly understood

the individual *in-force*, at the break up of the form, will "take hold" anew there where in the beginningless each-after-other self-attunement of the play of world-events, it can take hold—indeed, *must* take hold. This "taking hold" anew is not something that *has* law, that runs its appointed course according to definite laws, but it *is* law itself.

Now Kamma, as individual *in-force*, is a something unique. It is *itself* and nothing else besides, as it manifests itself in me the individual; for my consciousness tells me that I am a something unique, that I am myself and nothing else besides.

As a something unique, it must also be uniquely attuned to its new location. There will be one single location which, out of the endless host of world-events, will correspond to the Kamma of the disintegrating existence, will answer to it. *We all eat out of the one dish—every one eater for himself.*

This unique attunement, however, implies immediate passing over as a logical necessity. If Kamma passed over in space and time, this passing over would be a new self-attunement at innumerable points. Immediate passing over and unique attunement are two different expressions for one and the same event.

We shall have to dwell upon this idea at greater length in another place. Here I conclude with the

---

distinction between Sankhāra and Dhamma. The native scholars express this distinction by saying that the Dhammas take in, embrace, the element of Nibbāna. Which means nothing more than that they refer to *actual* processes, to living beings. Western scholars would do well to sit at the feet of the native scholars somewhat more than they at present incline to do. Many a misconception might thereby be removed, or prevented from ever arising, indeed. An admonition such as this is needed in every nook and corner of our literature upon Buddhism.

caution that the Kamma-teaching of the Buddha is not to be confounded with the teaching of the transmigration of the soul found in pantheistic systems. The two have nothing, absolutely nothing, in common with one another except the words "Samsāra" and "re-births." Language is no more than a servant. It serves one master just as well as another. To seek to deduce community of essence from similarities in terminology is a piece of idle trifling of which many an expositor of Buddhism is most unwarrantably guilty. It is no very difficult matter to "support" the words of the Buddha with quite a host of sayings culled from the works of mystics and pantheists—and scientists also, if one so chooses. But in good sooth, to him who understands, all this only makes needless ballast, and to him who does not understand, needless perplexity.

A transmigration of the soul requires something persistent, something eternal, a unity in itself. "As the worm from leaf to leaf"—runs the illustration in the Upanishads—"so goes the soul (the Atman, the true Self) from existence to existence."

For the Buddha there is no such "something in itself." For the real, genuine thinker life is a thing that at every moment wholly and completely arises anew. Life is this arising itself, just as a flame is the arising itself. *Any kind of persisting something here is not to be found.* Every moment of existence is a new, biological, Kammic value, whereof the prerequisite condition, the adequate cause, resides solely in the previous moment, while itself is prerequisite condition, adequate cause to the moment succeeding. *No continuity* is present, as a Being, as a true *I*, a something identical with itself, *but with each new moment the continuity is formed anew;* every moment is the last link in a beginningless series; every *now* the final result of an individual combustion process that, hither descended from past beginninglessness, continues to burn on through future endlessness; the Kamma whereof, as oft as one form falls to pieces, without break seizes hold of a new raw-material. It is no persisting something in itself that passes over; it is the individual tendency, the predispositions, the character, the consciousness, or whatever else one has a mind to call the value in potential energy represented by the *I*-process at its disintegration, that passes over, by *immediately* taking effect, striking in, imparting the new impulse to the material to which it is uniquely attuned—the material that appeals to it alone of all that is present, and to which it alone of all that is present, answers.

Yet once more:—

Kamma is no cord binding the existences together—as little so as the lightning of the firmament is a cord. The notion of a persisting "self" or "soul" is repeatedly and emphatically repudiated.

"Further, one may entertain the notion: 'This identical self of mine, I maintain, is veritably to be found now here, now there, reaping the fruits of its good and of its evil deeds; and this my self is a thing permanent, constant, eternal, not subject to change, and so abides for ever.' But this, monks, is a walking in mere opinion, a resorting to mere notions, a barren waste of views, an empty display of views; this is merely to writhe, caught in the toils of views"; runs a passage in the second Sutta of the *Majjhima Nikāya.* While we find Buddhaghosa's great commentary, the *Visuddhi Magga,* saying: "There is no entity, no living principle, no elements of being, transmigrated from the last existence into the present one."

. . . . . .

I sum up in brief what has gone before.

The Buddha teaches:—

All actual processes are combustion processes.

They burn in virtue of purely individual *in-forces* (Kammas).

As such they are self-sustaining processes.

As such they are beginningless.

They have sustained themselves from beginninglessness down to the present by volitional activities.

With the Kamma-teaching the significance of Buddhism for a world-conception is given in all its amplitude.

To possess a world-conception means to comprehend the play of world-events.

To comprehend means to comprehend adequate causes.

Adequate causes must be forces.

Forces of necessity must be something imperceptible to sense.

As such they must lie beyond the reach of all comprehension.

An exception to this is constituted by one single process—the *I*, the individual himself; inasmuch as the *in-force,* in virtue of which I have my being, *becomes* perceptible to sense in consciousness.

This given, the whole problem here focuses itself, as it were automatically, into one point, forth from which every genuine view of the world must necessarily proceed—*one's own I*.

Whilst faith conceives of the *I* from a transcendental standpoint, *i.e.* believes; whilst science strains itself to conceive of the *I* from the standpoint of the material world, *i.e.* inductively; *the Buddha conceives of it from the standpoint of itself*, i.e. *intuitively*.

Along with my comprehension of myself is comprehended the entire residue of the world. If I myself have being in virtue of a purely individual *in-force*, then all remaining actual processes also have being in virtue of purely individual *in-forces*, and I comprehend them all—*i.e.* the world—as thereby beyond being comprehended; not as being incomprehensible in themselves—that were a self-evident contradiction—but as so fashioned that each of them can only comprehend itself.

Here it may be objected:—

A world-conception that teaches me to comprehend the world as being incomprehensible—is it not just as much of the nature of a paradox as the world-conception of faith?

To this the answer is:—

The demand for a view of the world is not to be taken literally as such. If a freezing man says, "I much need a coat," it is not the coat in itself of which he has need, but the warmth that the coat will procure him. In the selfsame way, when an uninstructed person says, "I much need a view of the world," what he would fain comprehend is not the world in itself, but that which furnishes internal support, coherence, to the play of world-events. In reality, every world-conception means nothing else but a comprehension of the something that persists throughout the play of world-events, that remains constant through all vicissitude,—hence, a satisfaction *of the idea of conservation.*

This idea of conservation religious faith endeavours to satisfy with its "force in itself," God. Scientific faith endeavours to satisfy it with "matter," which is just as much a thing of faith as is "force." Actuality knows neither force by itself nor matter by itself; it only knows the unity of both: processes. One is just "believing" when one operates abstractly with either of these two opposites; and to operate with them other than abstractly is quite impossible.

Out of itself does science provide satisfaction for the idea of conservation in the cosmogony of energetics; this it does, however, by furnishing not *actual* energies but only the *reactions* of energies.

An *actual* conservation, and therewith an *actual* world-view is furnished by the Buddha alone when he points out that every living being is a something self-sustaining; in other words, that there is no such thing as an "*I*," considered as identical with itself, as a unity in itself.

The same, to be sure, is said by every school of criticism. Hume and modern psychology say so with unequivocal clearness, but none of them go beyond negation. They confine themselves to Socratic knowledge. Alone the Buddha says, "I not only am aware that I am no true *I*, as a unity in itself, but I also know what it is that I am. And that this has really been comprehended by me,—this I prove *in my own person.* For, from the moment that I comprehended myself as a process sustaining itself from beginninglessness down to the present hour by its own volitional activities, all volitional activities have wholly ceased in me. A new up-welling of *in-force*, any further self-charging of the *I*-process, has no more place in me. I know; this is my last existence. When it breaks up, there is no more Kamma there to take fresh hold in any new location, be it in heavenly, be it in earthly worlds. The beginningless process of combustion is expiring, is coming to an end of itself, like the flame that is fed by no more oil."

This thought which finds expression in the four propositions concerning suffering and the Nibbāna teaching, sums up the significance of Buddhism for morality and religion, and its amplification, therefore, belongs to the successor to this volume. Here it is only interesting to us from the epistemological point of view, *i.e.* in so far as *it makes ignorance as to oneself the antecedent condition of all life.* For—

I sustain my own existence through the perpetually renewed up-welling of volitional activities. It is possible for these to spring up again and again only so long as an object for my willing is present, *i.e.* so long as the delusion of identity is not put an end to. The moment any being arrives at the insight that there are in truth no identities—that there are nothing but flickering, flaring processes of combustion, which are one thing when I crave for them, another when I stretch forth my hand to seize them, and yet again another when I have seized them and hold them fast, he stops short, begins to reflect; and in reflection the blind impulse to live is sapped and weakened. The knowledge is borne in upon him: "It is not worth the seizing."

So long as I take a glittering object in the grass

for a diamond, I will clutch at it, scuffle for it—mayhap enter on a life-and-death struggle to obtain it. But the moment I perceive, "It is a dewdrop in which a sunbeam is reflected," I trouble myself no more about it. I know "A shake, a gust of wind—and all is over!"

So is it with the genuine thinker in face of the world and its values, whether they be called wife or child, money or possessions, fame or honour, family or home. One clear, piercing, scrutinizing glance is more than they will bear. To the penetrating mind, the wretchedness of transiency is everywhere manifest—he turns away—it is not worth while!

To Sakka, the king of the gods, the Buddha imparts the following instruction :—

"Then, chief of the gods, a monk hears: 'All that is, when clung to, falls short.' And when, chief of the gods, a monk has heard: 'All that is, when clung to, falls short,' he closely observes each and every thing. In the close observation of each and every thing he sees into each and every thing. And seeing into each and every thing, whatsoever sensation he experiences, whether pleasurable or unpleasurable, or neither pleasurable nor unpleasurable, in all these sensations he abides in the insight that they are transient, so that he cares naught for them, ceases from them, renounces them. And abiding as respects these sensations in such insight, he clings to nothing whatsoever in all the world. Clinging to nothing in the world, he is free from fear. Free from fear he attains to his own extinction of delusion." [1]

This insight that ignorance as to one's own self

[1] *Majjhima Nikāya*, Sutta 37.

is the antecedent condition of all existence, is formulated by the Buddha in the so-called "Causal Chain."[1]

It is not the intention of this book to furnish a fully rounded statement of Buddhism, and so I am at liberty here to confine myself to what is necessary for our immediate purpose. To attempt to deal in detail with all the many mistakes that have here been made by western expositors would require a whole book to itself.

The Causal Chain consists of twelve links, on which account it is also alluded to under the name of the "Twelve Nidānas."

The twelve links of the chain are: 1. Ignorance (Avijjā); 2. Predispositions, Tendencies (Sañkhārā); 3. Consciousness (Viññāṇa); 4. Individuality (Nāmarupa); 5. The seat of sense; 6. Contact; 7. Sensation; 8. Thirst of life (Taṇhā); 9. Clinging (Upādāna); 10. Becoming (Bhava); 11. Birth (Jāti); 12. A Complex consisting of the essential ingredients of all existence—namely, old age, death, misery, lamentation, sorrow, grief, and despair.

This "Chain" is translated by the great majority of occidental expositors of Buddhism thus: "Out of Ignorance arise the Predispositions. Out of the Predispositions arises Consciousness," and so forth.

Such a translation is at one and the same time incorrect as regards the wording and misleading as regards the meaning. For here the separate links of the chain are placed with regard to each other in the relationship of cause and effect, in the purely physical sense in which the two represent a follow-

[1] In Pāḷi, *paṭiccasamuppāda,* which may be rendered as "The together-arising in dependence upon."

ing after one another. But in order to have a pure following after one another of cause and effect, there are needed artificial preconditions such as physics puts for herself when she works with "bodies,"—that is, with fixed magnitudes complete in themselves. Actuality, however, knows nothing of any such things. Actuality knows only processes which at every moment of their existence represent a new biological value.

Only where "bodies" in this purely physical sense are presumed to exist, can one speak of a following after one another of cause and effect;—a mode of representing matters that is ridiculed by men of insight among physicists themselves. E. Mach, for example, makes fun of it in the humorous phrase: "Upon a dose of cause there follows a dose of effect"; whereby, to be sure, himself, and with him the whole of modern positivism whose mouthpiece he is,[1] falls into the opposite extreme, inasmuch as he seeks to substitute for the conception of causality of scholasticism—the following after one another of cause and effect—dependence outside of time, as represented by the concept of mathematical function.

In sooth, one position is as far removed from actuality as the other. Every causal relation existing in actuality runs its course on the lines—to take an example—of seed and tree, where the causal relation is neither a pure, unmixed following after one another, nor yet a lying alongside one another outside of time, but a combination of following after and lying alongside one another.

This combination of succession and juxtaposition

[1] Cf. Essay XI.

is implied, moreover, in the Pāḷi word, *paccayā*, used to express the connecting together of the separate links. Verbally correct and true to the meaning, the Causal Chain would be translated as follows :—

"Ignorance must be present in order that Tendencies may come to pass. Tendencies must be present in order that Viññāṇa may come to pass;—which latter here signifies Consciousness as passing-over Kamma; for this passing-over Kamma does not admit being spoken of otherwise than in the form of consciousness. This passing-over Kamma must be present in order that the fashioning of a new Individuality may come to pass. This latter must be present in order that a referring back of all the Six Kinds of Sense-Impressions to myself may come to pass. This must be present in order that Contact, an approaching on my part to things whether physical or mental, may come to pass. Contact must be present in order that Sensation, this in order that Craving, this in order that Clinging, this in order that the perpetually repeated, new upspringing of the *I*-process may come about which here is disintegrated in the stage of Passing-over (Bhava) and the final result (Jāti),[1] the Coming-

[1] The texts give the true meaning of *Jāti* with sufficient frequency, as, for instance, in the ninth Sutta of the *Majjhima Nikāya*, as follows :—

"Khandhānaŋ pātubhāvo, āyatanānaŋ paṭilābho, ayaŋ vuccat' āvuso jāti." Which means: "The coming into manifestation of the Khandhas (that is, the arising anew of corporeality, sensations, perceptions, discriminations, and cognition-acts, such as at every moment are exhibited in every individual combustion process, every alimentation process), the ever repeated seizing of the Ayatanas (that is, of the objects of sense, or of that, supported by which —in the objective as in the subjective sense—the senses are able to come into activity),—this, friend, is called birth."

I embrace the opportunity of calling attention to the equally misleading rendering of Nāma-rūpa by "name and form." The native pandits laugh at such a rendering. Here Nāma is "that which bends" (nāmeti), *i.e.* that which conglobates the material (rūpa) into that specific form through which even it becomes an individual. It is not merely name, but the totality

into-manifestation of a new Kammic impulsion *within* this my personality; whereupon the last link follows as a natural consequence.

The Causal Chain is the best touchstone by which to test whether a person is really capable of following the Buddha-thought or not. If he is incapable of doing so, he comes by a sad fall at the "violation" of the law of contradictories which follows from *Jāti* being taken as *Birth* in the grossly vulgar acceptation of the word; and cannot make out how an individual who has long since been active as such, should only subsequently be "born."

The other absurdity which necessarily arises when one interprets the links in the vulgar sense as a following after one another of cause and effect, is this: that in this case Ignorance is installed as a sort of blind end, and so the way is opened for the introduction of all sorts of cosmological speculations to which our men of learning are only the more inclined that they generally come from Sanskrit to Pāḷi, or, what in substance amounts to the same thing, from the Upanishads to the Suttas.

In the Vedanta, "Ignorance" is a given thing in itself, an incomprehensible; it is the point on which, for the genuine thinker, the whole system comes to grief. In Buddhism Ignorance is not anything that is given in itself. Its presence in everything that lives has no other basis than that

---

precisely of what most is worth naming. As a matter of fact, the pandits of Ceylon explain it as the evolutional form of Viññāṇa.

In harmony with this, in the above cited Sammādiṭṭhi Sutta, Sāriputta gives the following explanation: "Sensation, perception, volition, thought-contact, cogitation, this is called *nāma*." And in the Milinda Pañha it is said: "What is gross, that is *rūpa*; what is of fine, mind-like constitution, that is *nāma*." In the Abhidhamma exegesis, the so-called Nāma-series is directly identified with Viññāṇa.

all that lives, by the mere fact of its existence shows that it must have been compounded with Ignorance, since otherwise the *I*-process concerned would have been bound to have collapsed, just in the same way that everything that has being, by its very existence shows that up to now it must have been fertile, capable of propagation, since otherwise it could not be here. As little as on that account "fertility" is a given in itself, just as little is Ignorance a given in itself.

When the Buddha in the formula of causality places "Ignorance" at the head of his world-system, makes it the antecedent condition of all individual existence, he does nothing but formulate *abstractly* what in the Kamma-teaching he gives *actually*—the beginninglessness of the *I*-process. To the question, "What is the adequate cause of living beings? How is it ever possible for the *I* to come about?" he gives in the Kamma-teaching, the answer, "through willing," and in the Causal Chain the answer, "through ignorance as to one's self." Both answers bear the one import,—this, namely, that anterior to the present *I* ever and again stands the *I*, running backward in a series that knows no beginning, and never has known a beginning. Whether I say, "A being is here in virtue of his volitional activities, of his Kamma," or, "He is here in virtue of his Ignorance," there exists no other distinction between these two expressions than between the two phrases: "light is present," and, "shadow is present." Shadow in itself means nothing save only that light is present. Shadow is light itself, but in empty abstract form. In the selfsame way Ignorance of itself means nothing save only that will is present. Ignorance is will itself, but in empty abstract form.

In the intuition of the beginninglessness of the individual, both series—the actual as the Kamma-teaching, and the abstract as the teaching concerning ignorance—merge into one.

Buddhism is the teaching of actuality. The actual is only what I myself experience—I, the *I*-process.

The Buddha teaches me to comprehend myself, and only as a function of this self-comprehension does there follow a comprehension of the external world.

A view of the world based solely upon a comprehension of one's self perforce lies beyond reach of any inductive procedure; the question, therefore, arises :—

By what means and method is such a doctrine to be brought within reach of others?

VI

BUDDHISM AS A WORKING HYPOTHESIS

EACH with its own world-conception, faith and science alike, are representatives of a knowledge.

Faith stands for a "knowledge in itself,"—the knowledge, in fact, of a something divine. *Science* seeks to work her way to a knowledge placed in "law"; a labour, to be sure, with which she remains for ever "on the way." The *Buddha*, on the contrary, obtains his world-conception, not by the creation of any new knowledge *but by bringing to an end a beginningless ignorance.*

Now we moderns are accustomed to look upon science as the mediator betwixt us and truth,—as the high-priest of truth, so to speak, from whose hands we receive the sacred host. With the position which every science takes up towards nature—a rejection in principle of everything not perceptible to sense, implying thereby the potential comprehensibility of the phenomena of life—its methods also are definitely determined; they are the methods of *induction* and *deduction.* Both amount to comprehending an occurrence by roundabout ways through other occurrences; or, what is the same thing, to finding the adequate cause of one phenomenon of life in other phenomena of life.

Now there is one unique thing in the world with reference to which this possibility is absent—something that I never can approach by roundabout paths; it is my own consciousness. For, this I myself am; and where I am, thither it is impossible for me to go, though I seek so to do by the cunningest and craftiest of psycho-physiological by-ways.

The whole Buddha-thought has its roots in discernment as to the essential nature of consciousness. This discernment, however, is itself a form of consciousness, thus, cannot be come at by any kind of path, by any kind of method; *it cannot be mediate*.

Here the scientist will say, "If a discernment be not mediate—that is, derived from experience—then it must be immediate. But that means it is an illumination, a matter of faith. And thus the whole of Buddhism, with its teaching of Kamma, differs only in name not in nature from religions founded upon revelations."

Such a conclusion, however, would be false. There offers a third alternative.

Science conceals within herself a domain in regard to which it is with her much as it is with us all in regard to the sexual commerce of daily life. We are proud of our children but we are shamefaced over the act that has brought them into the world. Even so is it with science in respect of those of her children that have not originated as homunculi in the reagent tube, but have really been begotten—*her intuitions*. One is proud of them, but one never rests until one has methodized them, put the inductive smock-frock on them, and brought them into tune with the tone of conversation of science.

Galileo's law of falling bodies, the Newtonian law, Robert Mayer's law of the conservation of energy, are all intuitions. But many another flash of insight to which science has denied the status of legitimate child, contemning them instead for bastards, are like intuitions—such as the phrenology of Gall, Hahnemann's idea of *similia similibus curantur*, which has blossomed into the methods of treatment so fraught with blessing to humanity, of homœopathy, and many others.

All these intuitions have this in common that they have not been abstracted from a duly defined number of experiments. They are each an *experience* in the domain of cognition that has come to pass by reason of a unique impulse. They are each a process of mental growth, mental development that has been evoked by an impulse of a special character. As all vegetable growth demands an impulsion, a provocation, so also does that mental growth which science names "intuition." One does not arrive at an intuition by the paths of induction-deduction; one *grows* into it. Were the power of comprehending things so fashioned that it could lay hold of, work up, and assimilate a definite impulsion, as result there would blossom forth such a sequence as could never be reached by the path of experiment. A single impulsion, the lighter coloured blood of the venous circulation in the tropics, gave Robert Mayer his intuition. A single impulsion, a remark in Cullen's *Materia*

Medica about China and its characteristic of giving rise to intermittent fever, supplied Hahnemann with his intuition. A single impulse—so it is said—a falling apple, furnished Newton with his intuition; and so on through many examples.

Such an intuition is the Buddha-thought also. The sight of an aged man, a sick person, a corpse—so says the legend—gave rise in the Buddha to that impulsion which, worked up by him, and proceeding to bud and bloom, drove him forth from the home of his fathers, forced him into asceticism, eventuating finally the ripe fruit of the Buddha-teaching.

The Buddha-teaching is a pure intuition, is *the* intuition, and proves itself such in that any attempt to treat of it after the methods of science, to master it inductively, is impossible.

Though I lay the Buddha-teaching before the ablest scientific man that ever lived, it must always remain for him an entirely insipid thing if his intellectual faculty is not in such a condition as to vibrate in harmony with it, react to the "provocation" offered, work it up, assimilate it.

As little as it can be proven that a given food is nourishing for me—it can only be offered, and I myself must eat, whereupon the food of itself proves its own nutritive quality or its worthlessness—just as little can the truth of the Buddha-thought be proven: it can only be offered, and I myself must try it, whereupon the thought is either worked up as nourishing stimulus or rejected as entirely worthless. Here holds good the old saying: "*Sapere aude!*"

The Buddha-thought is powerless in respect of

a mind to which it is not assimilable, as also is that mind in respect of the Buddha-thought.

In respect of the teaching it is with such minds as it is with many desert regions of the torrid zone in regard to rain: their overheated soil prevents the rain-clouds that pass over them year after year from discharging their burden. They receive no rain, not because they are soaking with water, but because they are too parched and dry. They come under the law of the *circulus vitiosus.* Because they are rainless no vegetation can come; and because they are without vegetation no rain can come. Here there is nothing to be done but wait patiently until some time in the course of the beginningless, incalculable play of world-events a seed sprouts, a drop of water falls, and so a happier circle sets in which, with the increasing vegetation, increases the capacity for drawing down rain, and with the increasing rain-fall increases the capacity for bringing forth vegetation. In the selfsame way, in the case of those minds that are overheated with theories, there is nothing to be done but wait patiently, point out and point out again and again, until one day in the course of the beginningless, incalculable play of world-events some first grain of the teaching sprouts, some first drop of genuine insight falls.

Strictly speaking, no intuition, whether appertaining to the Buddha or to science, can be proven. All so-called proofs are surreptitious proofs, as is most clearly to be seen in the case of the scientific proof of the law of the conservation of energy. The value of an intuition admits of being measured only by its usefulness as a working hypothesis.

And so with respect to the Buddha-thought, the only thing to be done is to ask: "Of what use, of what service is it as a working hypothesis?"

If here it is of any service, a man will place confidence in it. If a man places confidence in it, he will reflect upon it. If he reflects upon it, he allows his thoughts to dwell upon it. If he allows his thoughts to dwell upon it, the more readily will the possibility occur of the mind leaping to the truth of the teaching and recognizing, "It is so!"

All mental life is based upon the thought-necessity of adequate cause. To it faith and science alike are subject. But no science is able to furnish any explanation as to what it is that this necessity is founded on.

The Buddha furnishes this explanation by showing that *consciousness—as Kamma—is this adequate cause itself.* Hence the necessity that wheresoever life runs its course under the configuration of consciousness, this question as to adequate causes is given along with it. So long as one fails to grasp the fact that consciousness is force, *i.e.* adequate cause, one seeks in phenomena that which one is oneself, that which is accessible nowhere else save only in oneself.

This it is which makes possible that scepticism—as found in Hume, for example—which denies that there is any *actual* causality at all. For the adequate causes of happenings can never *be proved,* since as forces they can never be perceptible to sense. From this there follows the possibility of unravelling a process to any extent one chooses without once coming upon anything to justify the conception of causality. One must first have understood that my consciousness, the consciousness of the investigator, is this causality itself, if one is to understand wherein lies the necessity of seeing a causal relation everywhere—*without seeing it!*

To arrive at the conception of causality by way of experience is quite impossible. This has been shown by Hume in masterly fashion. But his escape from the difficulty by declaring this conception to be a product of habit is all as mistaken as the other device of declaring it to be a something given *a priori* to all experience. There is a third alternative, lying between and above these two opposites.

As from the polygon one could never arrive at the conception of the circle, though one carried the duplication of the angles never so far—one would still be left with the concept of the polygon,—so from the simple data, from the following upon one another of two occurrences, one can never arrive at the conception of causality though one should multiply one's observations even to infinitude. One can only comprehend the circle from the polygon, when the former is given as ultimate concept (*Grenzbegriff*). In the selfsame way one can only comprehend the causal relation from the succession of events, when the former is given as ultimate value (*Grenzwert*). This, however, does not mean that it is a something given *a priori*; it only means that *consciousness itself is this ultimate value.* Towards this it is that all unwittingly one is striving when one sees in events the causal relation and yet is unable to furnish any explanation of it.

Such is the riddle of the *logical necessity of the law of adequate cause* as solved by the Buddha.

Again: All mental life splits itself up into these two divisions—faith and science.

Faith says, "There *must* be present a something imperceptible to sense." Science says, "We are unable to find anything imperceptible to sense and therefore reject in principle any such conception."

At this point the Master interposes and points out that they are both of them right, because they are both of them wrong, since neither of them knows how to interpret "consciousness," *i.e.* oneself. Consciousness, as Kamma, is the something imperceptible to sense, is the *in-force*, but it *becomes* perceptible to sense for me, the individual, in the course of its beginningless, self-acting development. Such is the interpretation supplied by the Buddha as to how it is possible for mental life to manifest itself in the two contradictories, faith and science.

Again: Science makes shipwreck on the boundlessness, so to speak, of her results. Make a beginning where she will, everywhere there opens before her a new, unending series of facts, each one of which in turn is the starting-point of another ınending series. And in science herself no point f departure is to be found, proceeding from which e might be able to account for this fact. She is ıble to say whether these series, converging, 'e on towards a conclusion, or the reverse.

Iere again the Buddha-thought proves its value vorking hypothesis.

e entire world of actuality consists of an ; number of self-sustaining processes.

The *in-forces* in virtue of which these processes subsist are imperceptible to sense, save where they become sense-perceptible to the individual himself as consciousness.

This amounts to saying that I can comprehend nothing but myself—that I can do nothing in regard to the external world but *react to it after a fashion altogether inexhaustible*—that, however, despite the endless diversity of the symptoms necessarily bound up with the same, a genuine comprehension ever remains equally near and equally far.

Whence, then, the fact of scientific law? For that science is in possession of genuine laws is proven by her faculty of calculating in advance. If, however, I can calculate in advance, this must mean that I not only react but also really comprehend.

It is precisely upon scientific law that a peculiar flood of light is thrown by the interpretation of the play of world-events yielded by the Buddha-thought.

Where the universe is nothing but an endless number of combustion processes, there the whole play of world-events is just the passage from one process to the next, the self-adaptation of process to process.

The play of world-events is law itself.

This, however, for the observing mind, also implies the possibility of apprehending the play of world-events as something that *has* law. As the flame *has* light and heat because it *is* light and heat—these themselves, so the play of world-events *has* laws because it *is* law itself. The laws of science are simply the outcome of an act of self-adaptation, self-accommodation to actuality. To use an illustration: Science in its relations to nature resembles an old body-servant who has studied his master's ways long enough to be able to prophesy with tolerable accuracy what his master will do then and then under this or other circumstances—provided only that he does not do something else!

Such is the position of science towards the inexhaustible play of world-events. The longer she observes, with all the more probability of being correct, she can tell beforehand what her master, Nature, will do at this or the other moment under such and such conditions—always supposing that he does not go away and do something else quite different!

All laws, even those that would appear to be most surely established, in every case hold good only up to the "now"; they may at any time be overthrown by the succeeding "now." Even the forecasts of astronomy—that pride of science—hold good always only under the proviso that the entire system within which the forecast applies, up till then has not suffered a collision; vulgarly put, that up till then the world has not come to an end. In fine, the forecasts of astronomy only hold good if something else does not happen, to say nothing at all of predictions in the field of biology, therapeutics, and so forth.

And so science hobbles along at the tail of the play of world-events, ever and again conforming herself to it anew, as she tinkers and patches up her "laws." And when she would fain have us believe that in the end man may soar to the position of lord of this world-process, she only resembles the fool in the Indian saying, who shakes his stick at the setting sun and then assumes great airs as if its going down was all his doing.

If one has comprehended the Buddha, one comprehends that the human mind can do naught save react in a manner that is altogether inexhaustible. As through and through a process of combustion, in every motion whether physical or psychical, I am this reaction itself. I am positively nothing else but just this reaction. The whole universe is nothing but an eternal self-adaptation of process to process.

Science in all its forms, without exception, is nothing but a methodical description of occurrences. All its "explanations," without exception, are only so many skilful forms of description.

When in hours of despair she now and then admits this herself, as Kirchhoff, for instance, has done in his well-known saying, this only means that she is making a virtue of necessity. And when E. Mach also, in his *Analyse der Empfindungen*, says: "One might imagine that the concern of physics is the atoms, forces, laws, that to a certain extent constitute the kernel of the sensible facts. Nothing of the kind! All practical and intellectual requirements are met so soon as our thoughts are able completely to counterfeit the sensible facts," he assumes with regard to nature the purely disinterested attitude of description, and in effect says the same as Kirchhoff.

It may be said:—

"Provided only that it were sufficiently abundant, might it not be possible through description also at last to attain to a genuine knowledge?"

To this the answer is :—

By description, even though carried on to all eternity, I attain nothing but the cognizing again and again of a certain occurrence as such, even under altered conditions, and in a state of disguise. But this act of recognition has nothing whatever to do with a genuine knowledge. I may meet a man year after year on the street, recognize him in every imaginable costume, be able to describe him with the fullest detail, all without knowing the man himself. And, to adapt this similitude to the Buddha-thought : Even if some day this man of himself should make himself known and say to me, "My name is so-and-so ; I am such-and-such a person," this would still mean nothing but an extension of the process of description. Really to know and comprehend means to know the energies at work in things. These, however, can be got at only in one single case : there where the individual comprehends them, *i.e.* in himself, in consciousness. Every other kind of intercourse betwixt me and the external world is all of it, positively all, nothing but a reaction. I can describe but I cannot explain, though I set myself to it never so scientifically. Though the intercourse betwixt myself and another be never so intimate the two *I*-worlds are for ever divided, the one from the other. Self-luminous and illuminating only oneself, each goes his own way through the beginningless infinitudes—a terrible thought when grasped in all its fullness. But it is verily so : actuality *is* terrible, and whoso fails to recognize it as such does not know it.

Here it may be interposed :—

"If each single person can do naught save react to the external world after his own individual fashion, how is it ever possible to arrive at uniformity in impressions, ideas, concepts?"

The answer is:—

By means of language such a thing becomes possible. Again and again language misleads us into thinking that solid bridges of thought stretch from *I* to *I*. But when I say, "That is green," "That is a tree," and so forth, and another person says the same, in strict truth we both agree only as regards the form of words. Each reacts in his own individual fashion, perceives his own "green," his own "tree." The Buddha instructs us that this individual perception and sensation also are merely forms of the individual combustion- or alimentation-process. These, too, are nourishment, a tasting, just like that of the tongue. *We all eat out of the one dish—every one eater for himself.*

"Whence, then, springs the uniformity found in our terms of speech?"

The answer is:—

Sounds are simply token-values. When I say, "That is green," the statement conveys no definite positive content of knowledge; in making it I only say, "That is not red, yellow, blue, and so forth." And if I say, "That is red," by such a statement I only say, "That is not green, yellow, blue, and so forth." Thus, just as in an algebraical equation, one sign repeatedly serves as the fellow-determinant of another, and none possesses any positive content of its own. Each merely announces that I react, *i.e.* that I burn. I do not recognize a cherry tree in itself, but only to the extent that it is not a plum or an apple or a pear tree, and so forth. And I recognize a plum tree just in so far as it is not a cherry or an apple or a pear tree, and so forth. It is a General Reciprocity Company, each member of which gives the other credit without a single member in the whole company possessing a penny of solid capital; in fine, a fraudulent concern which the honest, upright thinker must keep a sharp eye on if he would not be swindled.

"But whence comes language at all then?"

To this question the reply is: Thence whence I myself am come, whence thou thyself art come—out of beginninglessness.

The miracle of language is as little to be explained as the miracle of the *I*-process. There is present a given beginningless something—the world. And this thing given represents not only a mere *possibility*, as science would have us believe—whereby she lands herself in the predicament of being obliged to explain how all our faculties could have come to be—but it represents a *power* in itself, in which the power of speech is just as much implied, as a beginningless faculty, as the power to see, to hear, to think, and so forth.

I turn back to our main subject.

All the seeming explanations furnished by science are nothing else but more or less ingenious and special forms of description founded solely upon skilful adaptation. They assume the semblance of explanations from the fact that an impression of continuity is produced by an ever more closely packed accumulation of momentary forms. Such continuity, however, resembles the continuity of a circumference made up of a number of the smallest possible single parts: the greater the appearance of continuity, all the greater in reality, the discontinuity. The impulsion which furnishes the actual connection between events—the energies at work in occurrences, the real laws of formation—are thus never touched on at all, nay, they are deliberately ignored.

These eternally repeated attempts at adaptation on the part of science may very well be likened to the voyage of a vessel up stream through locks. When one has come to a stand-still in a lock—that is, when one has completed one act of adaptation—one waits until sufficient water—that is, sufficient new material in the shape of facts—has accumulated to enable one to reach a new lock—that is, a new act of adaptation.

This process of adaptation displays itself in its most characteristic shape when it assumes that epochal form known as "inversion of point of view."

An example of such an epochal form of adaptation to new factual material is to be found in the inversion that took place in the astronomical idea of the world when Copernicus displaced Ptolemy. A similar inversion, but in the epistemological domain, was effected by Kant, in terms of which the conformity to law observed in phenomena was lifted out of the occurrences and placed in the mind observing them. Another such inversion, but in the realm of biology, is the transition from the old teleological view which said, "The eye leads *to* seeing," to the modern mechanistic view which says, "The eye results *from* seeing."

It is one of the most striking proofs of how little

science is acquainted with her own nature that she extols these inversions as the greatest of her achievements. Far from that, they are nothing but the clearest possible expression of the fact that the human mind can do nothing but limp along in the wake of events; and as it does so, the incongruity, the lack of consonance, ofttimes becomes so very pronounced that nothing short of a complete revolution—some such inversion to wit—is needed every little while to relieve the situation?

Even the most successful of these inversions ever remains but an effort at adjustment. The Copernican inversion also is nothing but a useful "reading" of the facts of the astronomical world. When a sufficiency of new factual material has accumulated, then just as men perforce were swept away out of the Ptolemaic system, so in turn will they be swept away perforce out of the Copernican.

That whereby science finds herself constrained to make ever fresh adjustments, is experiment. With reference to this latter she resembles the neophyte in magic of Goethe's poem, with his broom. One is in danger of drowning in the superabundance of material, and knows not the magic word wherewith to bring the irresistible inflow of results to a stand-still.

Were the fresh facts which science is continually bringing forward real stages on the way to knowledge, then in the hour of death we could not help but feel like the expiring caravan animal in the desert, as with dying eyes it gazes after the caravan that wends its way there before it towards the longed-for goal now to itself for ever lost. Death to the thinker would be a most terrible occurrence, the hugest of all catastrophes. But science does not wend its way towards any goal at all. That question which science from her own resources can never answer, as to whether her endless series, converging, tend towards any goal, finds answer thus in the Buddha-thought: We can do naught save react, inexhaustibly react to the external world, and so doing we alike remain eternally near and eternally far from knowledge.

Science occupies herself with problems in variation and permutation. How were it possible for us to know so terribly much if we actually knew anything? Exact science has to do only with relations. She does not wish to know anything at all about things themselves. Any such knowledge would be as inconvenient to her as would be to an advocate a too far-reaching confession on the part of his clients. It is only this utter absence of misgiving as to things themselves which really makes possible scientific methods of procedure.

It is men of science themselves who are responsible—partly intentionally and partly unintentionally—for the mistaken, exaggerated ideas as to the nature and value of science current among the laity. One does not quite like to let people peep into pots. One much prefers to appear before an astounded public with results imposing by reason of their completeness. With a certain kind of diffidence—intelligible enough, by the way, to him who can see behind the scenes—which, however, with no little skill is so managed that along with the simple key-note quite half a dozen overtones vibrate in unison,—hopes, allusions to the future—one tenders one's gift to the world, but does not at all care about acquainting that world with the fact that at bottom this gift is the simple product of a scientific game of blind-man's buff, and "shut-your-eyes-and-hit-the-pot!" If it does not suit one way perhaps it will the other. Every theory is the outcome of trying, of testing. It was thus that Galileo himself adjusted his intuition with respect to the law of falling bodies. Thus did Kepler all his life "play" against nature and finally—once for all—win the game; and so to all eternity will this playing against, and these efforts at adjustment, go on. So to all eternity will descriptions in the form of explanations be brought forward—descriptions which, strictly speaking, will convey no more than Reuter's *bon mot* about destitution to the effect that it is the result of "poverty."

I can describe with increasing exactitude the fall of a body and formulate the laws that govern the same. But all these descriptive details only assume the character of an explanation through men in each case interpolating as adequate cause the attractive force of the earth. This latter, however, is purely the creature of thought, a working hypothesis pure and simple, advanced with the sole object of making possible the comprehension of all single instances of falling. From the purely epistemological point of view, I am equally entitled to say that the force of attraction results from the falling; for it is only from this, from a definite number of single instances of the same, that the theory of the "attractive force of the earth" is obtained.

With her working hypotheses science acts like a man who, in order to relieve himself of troublesome daily disbursements, pays out one lump sum of money for the settlement of all these petty claims. So science, in the place of countless daily, hourly—yea, in the amplest sense of the words—continuous incomprehensibilities of life, pays out one single, great incomprehensibility in the shape of central forces, atoms, ethers, out of which all the trifling requirements of the day—the running expenses, so to say—can now be met. The knowledge which science supplies us is the most pregnant possible expression for our ignorance. Were a genuine comprehension in question, one would make a speculation of it like a man who should buy up all the tickets in a lottery in order to make sure of the first prize.

From the position which science takes up towards the play of world-events—that of potential comprehensibility—she is obliged to combat everything that would militate against this potential comprehensibility. Hence the embittered fight over the axioms of mathematics. Science, if she would remain science, may tolerate only what springs from experience. But what springs from experience can also be swept away again by experience. As the god Kronos devours his own offspring, so, in reverse wise, does each young experience devour its genitor. But it is just this mobility, this, the complete relativity of her results, which lends to science her security. Were she anywhere to strike against solid ground, against anything not springing from experience, it would be with her as with a deep-sea vessel gone ashore: she would be dashed to pieces by the crashing waves of actuality. Of course there is no danger of any such thing happening so long as science keeps to *her own domain*, the re-actual world. As biology, however, where she must encounter life itself, face the fact *consciousness*, she is such a stranded ship as long since must have gone to wreck under the assaults of actuality did not physics time and again come to her aid and support.

This is the interpretation of the fact "science" in the Buddha-thought: We can do nothing but inexhaustibly react to a world which in its every motion *is law itself*, and therefore offers the possibility of a *reading in accordance with law*, but in regard to its own essential nature for ever and ever remains utterly beyond our reach.

Whence then the possibility of the human mind ever and again adjusting itself anew to this inexhaustible play of world-events?

Because thinking itself is energy, therefore it does not *have* the faculty, the power of adjustment, but *is* this power itself. Thinking in every form, even in the most vulgar, is a self-adjustment, and the scientific form is distinguished from the lay form only in this, that it is *directed*, set in play towards definite ends; hence, whatever is troublesome is here dropped with more skill, and on the doing of this, in the last resort, all scientific adjustment is founded. Rightly does E. Mach say, in his *Erhaltung der Arbeit*: "Science has almost made greater progress through that which she has known how to ignore than by that which she has taken into account."

Here for a first occasion I would bring that reproach against science which in what follows in treating of her problems will be frequently repeated: She deprives us of the sense of actuality; or, rather, places it in a false object, the re-actual, whereby she does just as much harm to honest thinking as faith does by placing it in a non-actual, in the transcendental.

There is only *one* actuality in the world—that which I experience as such. To deprive us of this pure actuality, to direct our attention towards a world that can be "read" in the form of work done —this I call a turning of genuine thinkers into tradesmen whose one and only concern is the establishing of advantageous relations with the external world.

Gradually to win back the lost sense of actuality, gradually again to arouse the feeling that there is a given something present which as such cannot be proven, not because unprovable in itself but because proving itself by itself—a given something representing no mere *possibility* but a *power*—this will be the first task of a time which itself feels in every nerve and fibre that there's something rotten. It is this blind running against all the facts of life, this courage of pure folly ever and again excited and supported by an overheated scientific imagination lacking in all self-control—it is this that we must leave behind would we make good our claim to be mentally adult.

That science can furnish no real explanations she herself admits with her calculation of probabilities on the one hand and her philosophy of probabilities on the other. Both require compromises with actuality, the ignoring of minimum values, the equating of an endlessly great probability with truth itself: in fine, an intellectual act of violence. Whoever has his need of a world-theory satisfied by Herbert Spencer's deductions, I should imagine he might also find it relieved by those of Thomas Aquinas. And if any one maintains with particular pride that his world-theory is based on strictly scientific axioms, he perpetrates an involuntary joke, inasmuch as he thereby says that his world-theory is based upon an exact calculation of probabilities; for, when all is said and done, the only exact thing about science is her calculation of probability—that is, the freedom she takes to herself to be inexact.

"What of mathematics?" it may be asked.

But the higher mathematics which, in the consideration of the world from the physical point of view, comes into question before everything else, is just the calculation of probabilities itself. And it is with no actualities that geometry and algebra deal, but with ultimate values—that is, values that are neither actual nor non-actual, but are given with actuality, as for example, the horizon and the ideal plane betwixt the air of the atmosphere and the surface of a sheet of water are neither actual nor non-actual, but merely things given with actuality.

This is a point of the highest epistemological importance which, so far as my knowledge goes, has nowhere been taken into consideration; to go into it more fully, however, would here be out of place. The Euclidean instruments—point, line, superficies—are simply, ultimate values of like kind; hence, neither actual nor non-actual. To operate with such ultimate values where the problem of life, actuality, is concerned, and in such operations to set out from mathematical truths, as does the Kantian philosophy for instance—this just means that one has failed to understand actuality.

Mathematics is only possible where there are identities. These, however, are to be found only in the realm of ultimate values. Actuality has no identities. Where there are nothing but combustion processes, there each moment of existence is a thing unique that never before has been and never again will be.

Whoso has comprehended the play of world-events after the manner of the Buddha, to such an one it becomes ever more clear that science, with her pretensions to furnish us at some future date with a genuine world-conception, resembles that penniless wag who affixed a notice outside his door bearing the inscription: "To-morrow I will pay my debts." Science, to the question as to when she finally means to pay what she owes to humanity, a genuine world-conception, has always but this *one* answer, "To-morrow!"

Science might easily obtain a clear idea of her own nature if only she would venture to think out to a conclusion her own trains of thought.

The nature of every scientific world-conception consists in comprehending the play of world-events in its entirety, without residue, as relation values. Herewith she remains stuck fast in what may be called conclusionless comprehension. The Buddha explains this fact in the manner already shown; science confronts this fact all uncomprehending of its import, and therefore with some show of justification can argue in this strain:

"We are undoubtedly making progress in comprehension, as is shown by our increasing capacity for determination in advance. Hence we are justified in presuming the final link in our train of thought—the entire play of world-events as a summation of pure relation values—and in building up for ourselves already the world-conception which we are sure to reach in practice some time in the future."

This is the world-conception which modern physics calls her cosmogony of energetics—that is, that ideal world which is wholly subject to the law of the conservation of energy, and thus is conceived of as consisting entirely of reversible processes not dependent upon time.

Of course, the more discerning among modern physicists now clearly perceive that the law of the conservation of energy merely represents from the limited standpoint of physics a *reading* of the play of world-events. If one forgets that, if one attempts to make it cover actual processes, tries to work it up into a world-theory, then not only does the real nature of the law of the conservation of energy come to light, but also the real nature of the whole of science. For—

The law of the conservation of energy has sense and meaning only in a closed system. In this fact alone its purely hypothetical nature already stands revealed; for never under any conditions whatsoever can actuality have a closed system. Thus at the very outset one has to make a compromise with actuality, a proceeding that is justified only where it is a question of achieving some practical result.

If now one makes the law of the conservation of energy into a universal law and on this erects a world-theory, one is bound to posit the universe itself as a closed system; otherwise, to speak of a universe in which the sum of all existent energies remains constant were altogether meaningless.

With this, however, science puts herself in such a position that, so soon as she ventures to think things out to a conclusion, she robs herself of the possibility of her own existence, as the following considerations will make evident.

A universe such as this, consisting entirely of relation values without residue, would be one huge process of compensation, an endlessly diversified fall from positions of higher to positions of lower tension. It is just this mode of representation which makes it possible for the physicist to calculate, to determine in advance. He cannot set about this his work at all until first after such a fashion he has given a new interpretation to the play of world-events. He must also, in similar wise, mechanise the invisible matter of the molecules, before he can master, so far as calculation goes, what takes place internally. In thought, one must loosen the existing connection between the molecules in order to be able to establish the internal falls. It is here as it is in a minuet: one takes a step backward in order to be able to take a step forward!

But this is what the physicist dares to do. All he is concerned about is to calculate, measure, determine in advance. As a general rule he not only says, "*Après nous le déluge*," but also "*Avant nous le déluge*." He rejoices in his power of being able to interpret and make use of the re-actual play of world-events to suit his own ends, and for the rest does not care a straw whence this power comes or whither in the future it may go. *He does not think: he only works.*

Now, so long as he preserves as physicist an attitude of strict impartiality towards this universe, the attitude of simple spectator, he may reach by calculation, by technique, whatever so is reachable. He stands before his universe as before an open piece of clock-work in which with increasing accuracy he observes the style and manner of its running and formulates the laws of the same. If, however, he allows himself to be led away into working at a world-view, into putting the question "Where will this clock-work run to?" he cuts the ground from under his own feet.

For in such a universe there remains as actuating impulsion nothing but the distinctions given with the separate processes. It is just like a pendulum ever hastening on towards a condition of rest.

Now, since under the assumption in question—a universe as a closed system—an influx of force from without is excluded, what we have here is a process of mutual borrowing, so to speak, and cosmic bankruptcy is only a question of time.

This logical necessity is taken account of by science in her entropy concept—the concept of the whole universe as a process hastening towards equilibrium, though that consummation be distant by millions of years.

Therewith, however—presuming that she is honest—science stands confronted by the following question:—

Every difference of tension demands a something that has established this difference. Where there is a swinging pendulum it must originally have received a push. If, however, the entire universe is one single mass of differences in tension, the impelling force can only lie outside the universe. In other words: this force could only have been the finger of a god. He it was, the Father-god, who put all his capital of force into this universe, upon which capital everything now feeds and will continue to feed until at length all is consumed, and the great world-death comes which "He" alone again can bid depart in communicating a fresh impulsion of motion—*if He should happen to feel so disposed.*

Of course science does not say, "Energy disappears." Instead she says, "Energy only becomes inert; *as such*, however, remains conserved." This, however, is about as sensible as if one should say, "Heat does not disappear, it only becomes cold; *as such*, however, it remains conserved" —an absurdity rightly denounced by thinking minds among physicists, such as E. Mach, for example.

And the conclusion of the whole matter?

The colossal achievements of science upon which is erected her cosmogony of energetics, have served no other purpose but to look after those interests of faith which faith itself dare not look after if it wishes to retain its vitality. In her audacious attempt to make light of the "imperceptible in itself," the god-idea, as a mere rudiment of atavism, science has made a pitiable shipwreck. By such an attempt she only shows that she herself is an apostate from the god-idea; and to be honourable, nothing is left her but to return as contrite vassal to the ancient and sovereign race of those that are "of Jehovah."

Should she, however, attempt to interpret the play of world-events not as a fall, but try instead to interpolate forces, then of necessity she must resort to the hypothesis of central forces; and, as above she plays into the hands of the extra-cosmic deity of monotheism, so here she plays into the hands of the intra-cosmic deity of pantheism; for this central force, if really believed in and not a mere working hypothesis, would be nothing else but the world-spirit of pantheism translated into physical terms.

These two, faith and science, at their deepest roots, share in one common nature, since both in truth represent that grandest form of symbiosis in which is made manifest the instinct of self-preservation on the part of the universe—the universe considered as the totality of all living beings. When faith thinks things out it falls back into the lap of science. When science thinks things out it falls back into the lap of faith. And both by their simple existence demonstrate the truth of the Buddha-teaching that all mental life perforce operates under the encumbrance of ignorance. For let science, or rather the scientist in person, place himself, if only temporarily and for a specific purpose, at the artificial standpoint of the mechanistic world-view, and so soon as he really begins to think he gives the lie to his own scientific view, inasmuch as he everywhere works with the concept of identity. Nay, he is never even in a position to maintain a clear distinction between the two points of view. This is proven by the problems of science, which, without exception, are of a purely dialectical nature, inasmuch as they all presuppose the erroneous concept of things as *identities*.

Our task here is to throw the light of the Buddha-thought upon these problems, and to this task we now proceed to address ourselves.

VII.

BUDDHISM AND THE PROBLEM OF PHYSICS

WERE one to lay the Kamma teaching of the Buddha before a physicist, in all likelihood he would dismiss it with this objection :—

"Immediate passing over that cannot be put to the proof in space and time is telekinesis. Telekinesis is a fact only for faith. Accordingly, Buddhism too, like every other religion, is a religion of faith."

The scientifically-educated man would probably concur in this train of thought. Hence, if Buddhism is to have any prospect whatever of playing a part in our intellectual life, it must offer a reply to such a line of argument.

That reply would run somewhat as follows :—

Actuality, when, where, and howsoever it makes itself manifest, really means nothing more than this —action is present. For actuality is action, doing, the power to do itself. It tells us, however, nothing at all as to how this action is bound to take place. Whence comes it then that science has the presumption to dictate to actuality a definite kind of action —would have it, so to speak, run along fixed rails ?

The one-sided requirement of science that all action must be mediate, demonstrable in space and time, follows perforce from the position she takes up towards nature.

Science is only possible where there is the perceptible to sense—where there is what can be compared.

Comparison is only possible where things are so arranged that the actual energies can be neglected. For every energy is something unique, strictly individual, not comparable, as my consciousness immediately proves to me.

This leaving out of account of the actual energies is only possible in the world of reactions. Here it is possible, and therefore also legitimate, to regard any kind of process as a something constant and complete, as a product, and correspondingly to treat it as such. Every physicist knows that the grocer's pound weight, as well as the grain of his own scales, rigorously tested, to-morrow are no longer the same as they were to-day. Nevertheless we make a compromise with actuality and act as though they were the same. It suffices for all practical purposes, and so is permissible. Here one is not at all aiming at a world-theory; one only seeks to measure and weigh, and satisfy certain needs.

This compromise with actuality—the looking upon things as finished, completed—is forced upon us by the idea of identity, with which all mental life, without exception, operates. And the physicist accommodates himself to this idea with his concept of "body."

Body, in the physical acceptation of the word,

is nowhere to be found in actuality; none the less the physicist is justified in making use of this idea so long as, in the pursuit of his aims, he can do so with advantage—that is, so long as it is a question of measuring and determining in advance.

The re-actual point of view of science involves as logical correlate the merging in one, of "motion" as manifesting itself to sense, and "energy." Aught else corresponding to energy besides motion itself is not to be found in the re-actual world of the physicist. Here motion is energy itself.

Under these two preliminary conditions—the regarding of things as "bodies," and their motions as energies themselves—the play of world-events displays itself in its entirety to perception by the senses; and every effect is something mediate, possible of being followed up in space and time.

But the movements that are perceptible to sense are just as little the energies themselves as "bodies," in the physical acceptation of the word, are actuality.

The sensible motion is not the energy; it is only the evidence that energies are present.

When two electro-magnets, placed in a certain position with reference to each other, go through circular movements, this does not mean that these circular movements are the energies themselves; it only means that energies are there present, and of themselves prove themselves such by producing effects.

When a geyser discharges water every hour, it does not mean that this kind of action is energy itself; it means nothing more than that energies *are there present*, and as such are at work.

The earth's course round the sun does not represent energy itself; it means nothing more than that energies are there present, and as such are at work.

Motion is not energy itself, but the by-product yielded by two systems of energies acting on each other. This by-product will manifest itself, according to circumstances and antecedent conditions, at one time as circular, at another time as elliptical, at another as rhythmical motion, and so forth.

In its essential nature this by-product—the movement perceptible to sense—corresponds wholly and completely to a shadow. As a shadow means nothing save that light is present—it is nothing but the by-product of two systems of energies, one giving, the other receiving, light—so "movement" means nothing save that energy is there present. It is nothing but the by-product of two systems of energies.

It is absolutely essential that the genuine thinker should make this idea as to the intrinsic nature of all motion his own. As little as it is possible ever to draw from shadows any conclusion as to light itself—saving the one conclusion that it *must be present*—just as little is it possible ever to draw from movements any conclusion as to the energies themselves, saving only that they must be present. The energies themselves withal remain wholly inaccessible. As to whether these are transmitted mediately or immediately, the fact "movement" supplies no information whatever.

Here the physicist will say, "That the movements are transmitted mediately is proved to me by experiment, since I can intercept an energy on its way at as many intermediate stations as I choose; hence, as mediate, can track its path."

But this is a grossly erroneous conclusion.

To be sure, if I have a magnet here and a needle there, I can intercept the magnetic energy at as many intermediate stations as I choose, and so construct for myself a "path" for the energy. But such a "path" is nothing but a dead line artificially made up of momentary reactions whose continuity is nothing actual and vital, but founded solely upon the minuteness and multiplicity of the moments of section.

Again the physicist may object:—

"We can measure exactly the speed with which the energies propagate themselves, as, for example, the time required for light to reach us from the moons of Jupiter."

But this also is an erroneous conclusion.

Of course, the fact itself is beyond dispute. But the time here mentioned does not represent the transmission-speed of the energies themselves; it only informs us as to how much delay these have encountered on their way; whether the halting-places have been very numerous and the stay at each a long one. This time which the physicist measures does not give the speed of transmission of the energies, but only the time of their non-transmission.

In accord with this is the incorrectness of ordinary physical terminology. The physicist calls light, heat, and so forth, energies themselves. But light is not energy itself, but only a designation for energies that lie for ever beyond our reach.

But once more I would call attention to the fact

that this entire manner of conceiving of things as "bodies," and of movements as energies themselves, is quite legitimate on the part of the physicist so long as he remains a physicist. It only becomes illegitimate when, reaching out beyond the field of reactions, it seeks to get itself recognized as a world-theory—that is, when it would have actual processes "read" in accordance with the like scheme. For now there follows the claim one makes upon nature that all her action shall manifest itself mediately, as possible of being followed up in time and space.

The illegitimate feature about this conception arises from the fact that it poses itself with an insoluble problem—the problem of telekinesis.

If one regards things as "bodies" in the physical sense, and if upon this conception one insists on erecting a world-theory, then one has to solve the question: How can it ever be possible for action to take place between separate bodies?—a question which involves the idea that every effect produced by contact, even the very slightest, always presents itself to thought as a form of telekinesis. In other words: Everywhere effects are being produced, and yet one is unable to explain how they can ever be brought about.

The insolubility of this problem is attributable not to things but to thinking; that is to say, it is a problem of a purely dialectical nature.

In starting out from the conception "body" as a thing complete in itself, identical with itself, one cuts oneself off from the possibility of ever being able to explain how one thing can act upon another. In thought one has torn things out of their natural connection, and holds them fast conceptually in this artificial isolation. Once I make a thing a "body," no power in the world can move it so as to bring it into contact with some other thing; as little so as any power in the world can impart movement to a reflected image, taken by itself. Just as such movement can only be brought about through movement of the object reflected, only from this can proceed, so contact between things can only take place, proceeding forth from the beholder, when he lets drop his false notions and comprehends actuality unmodified as that which it is—namely, *perpetual coming together into contact itself.* Actuality is verily nothing but the passing over from thing to thing—that is to say, process. Actuality is not, as science would fain have us believe, mere *possibility*—if so, it would always be necessary first to have explained how these possibilities could ever arrive at realization—but actuality is a *potency*, and so, at every moment of existence, self-realization itself.

If only actuality is rightly conceived of, the question as to how action betwixt thing and thing can take place simply loses all meaning. Actuality is seen to be nothing but this action itself. Where one is, thither one cannot go; and what one is, that none can become.

When physics, and with it science as a whole, puts forward the claim that all action must be capable of being tracked mediately in space and time, it excludes itself from this requirement. For, without exception, every case of action in its own domain is to be read as a special instance of telekinesis. But be it well noted, the concepts, action by contact and telekinesis, are not something existent in themselves; they are merely intellectually-conceived functions of the purely artificial concept "body." Where this concept is absent, there is neither action by contact nor yet telekinesis; there the whole universe, as a totality of combustion-processes, is action itself, but tells us nothing whatever as to how action can come about, or as to whether this action is mediate or immediate.

How action proceeds can never be comprehended from the observation of reactions, though one should track these with never so much perseverance and accuracy; that can only be ascertained where one is acquainted with the energies themselves.

In all the world there is but *one single* energy that is open to approach—my own *in-force* which *becomes* perceptible to me in consciousness. Thus the question as to how action itself proceeds can never be answered on the lines of induction: it can only be *experienced.*

When one asks the Theras of Ceylon for an illustration of how Kamma passes over from one existence to the new location, the example of teacher and pupil is that most frequently given. As instruction, stimulation, pass over from teacher to pupil, with effects that last throughout the latter's entire lifetime, even so does Kamma pass over.

And just here we come upon something that lies too close at hand for the ordinary person to give much heed to it. Nothing is more strange to us than actuality—that is, than we ourselves!

As a matter of fact, life in its entirety, as it runs its course among human beings, is such an instance of immediate effectuation. All actuality is immediate: it is only *re-actuality* that is mediate. Wherever I actually am alive, I stand in the midst of such immediate effectuations as mock at all scientific calculations.

When two pairs of eyes encounter one another and that springs up which we call love or hate, as the case may be, this is an instance of immediate passing over between two systems of energies. All forms of mental excitement, all our numberless sympathies and antipathies; the mutual understanding between man and man, between man and animal; the unspoken self-revelation, self-discovery between man and wife; the communion between mother and child;—all these are immediate effectuations. Each possibility of one giving an order to another, of one obeying another; all possibility of life in communities, animal or human; every possibility of education, has its roots in such immediate effectuations. But the very attempt to enumerate them tends to beget the fallacious idea that they are the exceptions. It is not so! All beings communicate with one another immediately. In immediate effectuations we live, move, and have our being. But through the re-actual apprehension of things inculcated by science our sense of actuality has become so dwarfed and stunted that we no longer dare to take actuality as itself; nay, we do not even know how to do so, but are disposed to recognize it as such only when we can have it handed us by some system of grains, feet, and seconds.

All unspoiled, natural thinking and feeling proceeds by way of immediate effectuation. The never wholly-eradicable idea of magic, as it still survives to-day—one last little remnant of it—in the form of "*Sympathiekuren*," is nothing else but the instinctive idea of the necessity for such effectuation. How the nobleman of Capernaum would have laughed if Professor X. had said to him, "When you say to your servant, 'Do this!' and he does it, that seems to you quite a natural thing. But in strict truth this fact simply bristles with insuperable difficulties from the point of view of exact scientific explanation." It is the high privilege of our age to listen with becoming awe to such-like profound absurdities just because the sense of actuality is lost to us, because through the insistence and authority wherewith science has been able to make her re-actual views prevail, we have finally come to the point of believing in all seriousness that in the actual, in things like eating and drinking, a proceeding indispensable to their proper performance is carefully to count one, two, three!

Science dubs all immediate effectuations "mystical," and refuses to rest until she has extirpated all such-like ideas. But the mystical is not that which science understands by the term; for to her the mystical is nothing but the non-scientific. It is actuality itself that is mystical. Apart from actuality there is nothing mystical whatever; for it is only the actual, no matter where one lays hold of it, that rolls back into the twilight of beginninglessness. Beginninglessness is what is mystical, and my consciousness *the* mystical itself. A miracle is nothing mystical. For, if it happens, then it is law; and if it does not happen—why, then it simply is not!

This immediate action of man upon man—this it is that reveals to me how energies operate. When a glance from my eye produces a "stir" in another human being, this energical impulse is not obliged to pass through all the media lying between, but operates *immediately*. To be sure, an attempt is made to read mechanically this fact also—to interpret it in the form of psychic vibrations, subtlest etheric waves; and science and theosophic, spiritistic, and all sorts of mysticism here go hand in hand. But there is not the least necessity that it should be a glance, a sound, or anything else of a positive nature which moves another. A silence, a failure to look may ofttimes be that which produces the most striking psychic convulsions. To interpret this, however, as a case of transmigrating vibrations, were scarcely possible even for the boldest of hypothesis-makers.

It is even so! That which is most natural is most strange to us. Here too, as with "consciousness," it is a case of *sapere aude!* We simply must learn again to dare to take actuality for that which it is—for that which acts there where it can and must act.

When love springs up between two beings, this means that unique attunement prevails. This, however, signifies that energy passes over immediately. It has no need first to wrestle with air and ether molecules: *it exists there only where it acts, and it acts there only where it is uniquely attuned.*

This is the way in which actual energies operate. This way cannot be proven inductively: it can only be experienced intuitively. And it is this experience which supplies us with our parallel, our point of support, in comprehending how Kamma works. And only because we have lapsed out of this actual life into the re-actual life of science, has the Kamma-teaching become strange and unnatural to us.

The value of an intuition to him who has not himself experienced it, is only measurable by the extent to which it is of service as a working hypothesis.

Of what service is the Buddha-thought here?

In the first place, it makes it possible to "read" both kinds of motion, the inorganic as well as the organic, the falling as well as the proceeding, from one common point of view.

Where the whole *actual* play of world-events is a summation of self-sustaining processes, existence is action itself; and the simple existence of an energical, of a Kammic system, purports that it makes itself felt with regard to other systems of energies—sustains itself in opposition to them. Actuality is devouring: man in his very nature an eater.

Where there are a number of energical systems, they act against one another. Where there is action, the corresponding reactions are present in the shape of motions perceptible to sense.

These latter, here also, signify nothing save that energies are present, and as such are at work according to circumstances and antecedent conditions.

When two men, in wrestling with each other, fall into a whirling movement, this by no means implies that there resides in these men an energy of this particular variety; it means nothing more than that energies are present, even as the circular movement of two electro-magnets intimates nothing more than that energies are present. Here also motion is only a by-product, the equivalent of the shadow in the case of light—nothing in and of itself. When the flower unfolds itself to the sun, when the creeper draws itself up towards the light, when the caterpillar crawls along the leaf, when the wild geese cleave the air like a wedge, when the dog snaps at the tit-bit, when I lift my arm, lie down, get up, do this or the other thing—in each case it is the same. All this only intimates that energies are present, and in the course of their action against other systems of energies yield by-products. In this mode of apprehending the fact "motion" as the *shadow of energy* the entire play of world-events, organic as well as inorganic nature, the dead as the living, the re-actual as the actual, admits of one uniform reading.

Secondly:—

In her fight against "telekinesis," it is with science as with one who in public discourses eloquently on enlightenment, but whose own house is haunted by a ghost.

This hobgoblin of exact science is *gravitation*; and it bids fair to scatter all exactitude to the winds, since the physicist, too, is unable to represent it to himself otherwise than as acting independent of time.

In the Buddha-thought this independence of time permits of being "read" without the least difficulty, since here it is nothing but the by-product which two systems of energies acting upon one another yield with every alteration of energy-value on one side or the other. When I shift the light with reference to the object illumined, the movement of the shadow takes place as a by-product independent of time. In the selfsame way, what we call gravitation is nothing but the by-product independent of time which informs us that a change is taking place in the energical relation of two world-systems.

Thirdly:—

The Buddha-thought furnishes a reading of the concept of time and space.

Time and space as something existent in themselves are only possible where one is working with "bodies" in the physical sense, where one is operating with identities. Such bodies have need of a space existent in itself in order to perform movements; and, as a matter of fact, physics so completely objectifies the conception of space that it does not hesitate to make the attempt to determine the curvature-measurement of space. Such bodies, further, require time as something objective in order to traverse this space. An objective time and an objective space represent, so to speak, the ordinate and abscissa of the artificial system "body" as conceived of by the physicist. If one does not work with such "bodies," but, as a philosopher, with things regarded as mere "appearances"—like Kant, for instance—then time and space, from being things purely objective, must become just as much things purely subjective—forms of perception given *a priori*; the one view as erring as the other!

"Avoiding both extremes, the Buddha points to the truth in the mean." This continually-recurrent phrase applies, as everywhere, so also here in the strife of opposites. Actuality has no opposites. It is the union of opposites itself. And wherever contention reigns of or about opposites, it only shows that both parties alike have become entangled in pseudo-problems of a purely dialectical nature. This the seeker for truth may depend on, as a rule that has no exceptions: Where there are opposites, there is nescience! Whence it follows that there is no solution from the side of things, but only from the side of thinking, in the rectification of our mental assumptions.

So also is it here.

Where the actual play of world-events is comprehended as a summation of individual combustion-processes, time and space are things neither purely objective nor purely subjective, but belonging equally to both—a *Becoming*, like everything else. They arise, spring up, in the effectuation of the *I*-process with respect to the external world wheresoever the preliminary conditions are such that they can and must unfold themselves; in just the same way that consciousness arises in the effectuation of the *I*-process with respect to the external world wheresoever the preliminary conditions are so regulated that it can and must unfold itself.

So much for the Kamma-teaching, and its bearing upon the claims of modern physics.

Immediate passing over does not contradict actuality, but only the artificial premises of science. All that is actual is immediate. For this reason a passing over of the actual in time and space is an absurdity, since time and space are, first and foremost, functions of the actual, forms of experience, hence never can be made to serve as measure of this experience.

VIII

BUDDHISM AND THE PROBLEM OF PHYSIOLOGY

In the position it assumes towards actuality science resembles a man who has reduced all language to mere grammar and now finds himself hard put to it to explain how purely grammatical signs and formulae could ever have given rise to actual speech. As grammar presupposes actual speech—is secondary, derived from it—so the mechanical, re-actual view presupposes actuality—is secondary, derived from it—and it is against all common-sense to seek now to turn the tables with an endeavour to prove the possibility of the living language "actuality," assess its title to existence, by the "grammar" of the scientific conception of things. From this position, the fact that anything ever happens at all, remains an eternally unfathomable mystery.

The first claim upon the genuine thinker is that he should understand clearly that a something given is present, whose simple existence represents also the *power to exist*; whose activity has no need of being proven, since proving itself by itself. The endeavours of science from its re-actual position, to govern and administer actuality itself also, betray a limitedness and crudity of thought at which later generations will stand amazed. So long as science fails to understand and respect her natural limitations, so long as she keeps trying to interpret the actual mechanically, so long is she as serious a danger to the world as faith.

In the treatment of the problem of physiology that follows I can be brief, because all the details here relate to a technical domain to which the majority of my readers are unlikely to bring either interest or ability to understand.

Just as physics—in the widest sense of the word—may be briefly designated as the teaching that informs us of the relations existing between "bodies," so physiology may be succinctly termed the teaching that instructs us as to the relations existent between living beings and the external world.

Where living beings are comprehended as processes of combustion pure and simple, every relationship betwixt them and their environment becomes a *form of alimentation.* The intellectual as the vegetative, the psychic as the physical life, are here comprised under the one common, all-inclusive concept of alimentation. Whether I appropriate, assimilate something to myself through the organs of sense and thought or through the tongue and the digestive apparatus, both proceedings are the same—forms of alimentation.

Accordingly we find the Buddha calling living beings "āhāraṭṭhitikā," *i.e.* "existing through alimentation," and placing this expression—as synonymous—alongside "sañkhāraṭṭhitikā," *i.e.* "existing through Sañkhārā," compounded, conditioned.

Here in their every movement the entire existence of living beings becomes a *laying hold of the external world*—a gross laying hold with hands and teeth as well as that subtle *mental* laying hold which we generally denominate "comprehension." As the whole existence of a flame is a laying hold of the external world, as it subsists solely by reason of this prehensile activity, even so is it with the *I*-process.

Buddhist psychology distinguishes between four varieties of aliment. First, there is aliment in the common, vulgar sense of the word, be it in gross growth-promoting form as solid or liquid food, be it in fine growth-promoting form as respiration. Second, contact, as the mutual encounter of the senses and their corresponding objects. Third, mental apprehension; and fourth, consciousness; these two latter being the working up, the assimilating of what issues from contact.

From the commanding height of the position which Buddhist thinking takes up towards the process of life, it cannot possibly encounter that "problem" with which scientific physiology finds itself forced to wrestle.

Briefly stated, that problem runs as follows:—

"How can it ever be possible for a living being to appropriate something to itself, assimilate something, take up something into itself, whether this 'something' be of the gross growth-promoting variety—nourishment in the vulgar sense of the word—or of the intellectual sort, as sense impressions and the content of consciousness?"

There was a time in the history of natural science, more particularly in the history of the healing art—and that time is hardly past yet; we still stand within its fringes—when to work at all with the concept of a "vital energy" was regarded as synonymous with being unscientific, indeed, was esteemed mere blind faith. At every opportunity, seasonable and unseasonable, it was declared that "to-day" we had no longer any need of a "vital energy," that the mechanical view explained all that very much better; yet, in actual truth, one only showed how wanting one was in the sense of actuality when one could accept as satisfactory a "reading" of life which presented it under the figure of endosmotic and diosmotic processes, and such like.

Here, however, is abundantly proved true that saying of Horace that nature is something which man cannot drag out even with a pitchfork; and it was with a pitchfork of the biggest sort that the mechanists took the field against actual life. To-day the antithesis of the mechanical view—the teleological—has found its way back into medical thought, and begins again to move about naturally and without restraint in the domain of therapeutics.

Beyond all else, it was the progress made in physiological chemistry, the peculiar, seemingly inexplicable facts here observed, which perforce impelled towards this inversion of positions.

Here in the domain of physiological chemistry there come to light processes, reactions, which make a mock of all the rules and laws got from re-agent tubes. Here in the living organism it is found that the "strongest" acid—sulphuric acid—is crowded out of its combinations by the "weakest"—carbonic acid; which means nothing else but that the concept of "strength" as it has been taken over from inorganic nature does not apply here at all. By reason of such experiences it has been found necessary to introduce a new concept, that of "avidity"; in other words, here as everywhere, one hobbles along at the heels of the facts of actuality, being obliged ever and again to adapt oneself to them anew as best one may.

Here in the living organism, albumen, fats, and carbohydrates are worked up at temperatures at which they undergo no change under the action of the oxygen of the atmosphere. The most marvellous thing of all, however, is the action of the glands, which, in taking up the material to be elaborated, display a power of choice that, so far as our ideas go, defies all explanation. Not the least regard is here paid to chemical and physical laws as abstracted by science from inorganic nature. Complete arbitrariness prevails. The epithelium of the stomach, for example, possesses the power of always despatching the hydric chloride set free from sodium chloride in one direction—namely, into the excretory ducts of the rennet glands, and of always sending the sodium carbonate formed in another direction, back into the lymph and blood circulation.

Examples such as this might be multiplied to almost any extent, did we here aim at completeness.

The key-word to it all, as revealed to us by the latest researches in physiological chemistry, is—arbitrariness!

Of course, as everywhere so also here, only give her time enough and science will come round to adjustments in thought, and with that to the formulation of all such facts into laws. In respect of such facts, however, it must clearly be understood that the purely mechanical view is no longer able to hold the field; that the teleological view has broken through the artificial embankments of the mechanical view and again poured forth over the level lands of scientific thinking.

That which has hitherto given such weight to the mechanical view in physiology is the possibility, up to a certain degree, of reading the physiological facts mechanically. One can "read" the eye so far as its external apparatus is concerned, according to the laws of catoptrics and dioptrics; but the bearing of this upon the faculty of seeing or upon an explanation of that faculty is simply nothing. This is not the fitting place to deal with the revolting outrage upon sound thinking of which the scientific theory of vision is guilty in its interpretation of the reversed retinal image: that demands a chapter to itself.

One may "read" the heart and the vascular system as a pumping contrivance, and the osseous system and its joints as an arrangement of levers. One may reckon in heat-units the nutrition-values taken in and given off, and equilibrate them with tolerable success, as can also be done with a calorimeter; that is to say, one can "read" the living organism in accordance with the formula of the law of the conservation of energy. But nothing thereby is gained that is of the slightest assistance towards a comprehension of the *actual* energies at work in all these functions, except in so far as to the genuine thinker all this makes more vital and pressing the question as to what precisely that wonderful something is which pulls the strings. And if one school of science would like to make us believe that on the basis of an ever-increasing facility in "reading" the organism mechanically the question as to actuating energies may in the end be completely disposed of, as referring to quantities so minute as to be negligible, it need not be taken seriously; it only resembles a man who would account for the revolution of a wheel solely from the shape and texture of the wood.

That which along with the results of physiological chemistry helped towards the overthrow of the mechanical view, was the new tendency in therapeutics—serum therapeutics, to wit—which, put briefly, amounts to a working out of specific affinities between the living organism and certain organic substances.

As the physiological chemist was forced to note that he had fallen out of the realm of crude but easily-handled quantities into the realm of unaccountable qualities—that is, out of re-actuality into actuality—so was it with the experimenter in these specific remedies. One was obliged to take note that in this field the grossly quantitative according to mass and weight no longer went for anything. Ehrlich calls the antitoxins "magic bullets" which hit their mark *immediately*. Here it is no longer a question of the mere more or less by which one has hitherto been accustomed to gauge effects, but of an attunement more or less fine and delicate. In short, one has forced one's way into the domain of actual energies and seeks gropingly after one or another method of accommodation. For the quantitative position may not be abandoned entirely if one would remain scientific. One must be able to measure. Actual energies, however, do not admit of being measured by dead material. They are only to be measured through themselves, *i.e.* through their working.

Already more than a hundred years ago, Hahnemann, the founder of the homœopathic method of treating disease, consciously and completely abandoned the crude quantitative position in the field of medical science. He had freed himself entirely from the quantitative conception of curative effect. He called his remedies "potencies," and this potency was determined not according to mass but according to the fineness, the delicacy of the mutual accord between the organism and the remedy. This mutual accord, however, grows subtler, more acute, with progressive dematerialization, with the freeing of the active energies resident in the remedies from the burden of their ballast of material. Hence the apparently paradoxical idea that the curative effect augmented with the diminution of the dose—an idea which has given the doctors of the orthodox schools such abundant occasion for misunderstanding and barbed raillery. The effectiveness is not increased with the lessening of the dose, but with the subtilization of the unique accords concerned. Hahnemann had the courage to bring his thinking into line with the actual energies and their manner of working—a courage which modern serum therapeutics does not possess, and quite likely never will possess, so that we may look to see the wave of actuality which here has burst upon therapeutic life again crushed under by re-actual tendencies.

Wherever opposites are found, there mere dialectical problems form the subject of contention. The contradictions between the mechanical and the teleological views with respect to the living organism are also of a purely dialectical nature. Both take up the position that the organism is an identity, and accordingly a something so constituted that it can take nutriment *into itself*. Both alike, teleology as mechanism, looking upon the cell as life itself, make it their endeavour to master the miracle of that life; the former, as a result of its efforts, coming to the conclusion that a vital force, an incomprehensible something in itself, must somewhere lie concealed in this wonderful machinery; whilst the latter pushes on unswervingly towards the goal it has set before itself—that of becoming, by ever closer and closer description, master at length of the great riddle.

As everywhere, so also here, the Buddha stands between and above these two opposites, inasmuch as he teaches:—

A living being so constituted that it must and can take up something *into itself*, simply does not exist. Such a living being is only to be found where one is dealing with the concept of identities. But identities are nowhere to be found within the domain of actuality. Here are only processes of combustion. If one sets out with the concept of identities, one creates for oneself a problem whose insolubility proceeds as much from its purely dialectical nature as the problem of telekinesis in physics. If one abides by the *actual*, if one holds strictly to the insight that living beings are individual processes of combustion, then there exist nothing but energies which for a certain period of time put a body of material specifically belonging to themselves in a specific condition of tension, for a time maintain it so, and then after a time again abandon it. Here the cell is not life itself, but simply the most primitive structural expression of the fact that certain materials find themselves in a certain state of tension, in the same way that the ridges and furrows in a Chladni's sound-figure are a structural expression of the fact that a certain material—some sand on a glass plate—finds itself in a certain state of tension.

This whole body of phenomena is by physiology termed the "circulation of matter." But there is here no "*I*" as an identity that takes up matter into itself, melts it down, and—so to speak—gives it forth again as new coinage. Nowhere in the universe are there any unstamped values, nowhere is there any raw material of substance, but always and everywhere only a recoining: a continuous change in the individual conditions of tension which as little warrants the idea of "resorption"—taken literally—as the flame, or the wind that for a certain space of time whirls up and holds a certain particle of sand in a certain form. An appropriation, a taking up into oneself, can only take place where there is a proprietor able to take something into his house. But actuality does not permit of any such comfortable ideas. Here are nothing but energies that continuously lay hold, pull to themselves, and maintain what has thus been pulled, under the influence of their individual tendency, until such time as other energies make their presence felt in superior force, whereupon the tension is dissolved here, only to assert itself anew elsewhere.

Whatever may be manifest as form in the living being, from the gross forms of the limbs down to the cell, to its protoplasm, to its nucleus, to the ever-new marvels of the structure of its body—it is all alike one material, maintained by one individual energy in an individual state of tension.

I do not *have* the marvel of alimentation as my function, but I *am* all this itself; and beyond this, nothing! That, however, I am this individual, unique being—of this the antecedent conditions lie buried deep in beginninglessness.

Kamma is an individual energy: as such it is a thing unique: as unique it seizes hold of Kammic, *i.e.* unique material, whereof the uniqueness is proven in the fact that Kamma evolves therefrom a unique being, an individual. If all this marvel of alimentation, this marvel of sight, hearing, and so forth, were obliged to come about as a something entirely new only through external preconditions, never could it come about at all. I learn to see, hear, taste, and so forth, as the flame learns to burn, the flower to blow. All this, down even to the minutest detail, lies ready, prepared beforehand, in the material; and it needs but the stimulator—which, just because it is a question of a unique material, must also be a thing unique—in order to have all these properties brought into play, have them set in full activity.

The material lineage of the living being is perforce as beginningless as the Kamma lineage; but whilst the beginninglessness of the latter manifests itself only immediately in consciousness, the beginninglessness of the former admits of being comprehended only mediately as a logical deduction.

"Suppose, O monks, that a man were to cut down all the grass and leaves in this Jambudīpa [India], and, gathering them together, take one handful after another and say (at each handful), 'This is my mother; this is my mother's mother,' there would never be any end to the mother's mother of such a man; but all the grass and leaves in Jambudīpa well might run out, well might come to an end."[1]

Both lineages, the material as the Kammic, are a beginningless, reciprocal, each-to-other self-attunement, in a universe that in its every motion is law itself.

To this we shall have to return in the succeeding essay, in treating of the problem of heredity.

The man of science will say, "It is no very difficult matter to explain everything if one simply refers everything back to beginninglessness, and assigns as reason for the fact that everything is as it is, that in accordance with the natural conditions of growth it has been *obliged* to come about thus and not otherwise."

To this it may be said in reply that the Buddha-"reading" of the play of world-events is productive of but little for science, being that reading which is actuality itself—which takes and leaves actuality as that which it is, thereby shutting off the very possibility of all those learned and profound researches which accrue to science in such abundant measure through its endeavours to have actuality become actuality only under its own hands, so to

[1] *Samyutta Nikāya*, ii. 15, 3.

speak; in somewhat the same way that I, the living being, exist to a magistrate, not as myself, but only in virtue of certain identification papers.

Besides, the Buddha-thought is an intuition. And the value of an intuition is made manifest solely in its use as a working hypothesis.

As a working hypothesis, then, of what service is the Buddha-thought in the domain of physiology?

The answer is:—

It alone explains the possibility alike of disease and of cure.

Neither for science—that is, in the purely mechanical manner of regarding the living being—nor for faith—that is, where living beings are represented as endowed with soul—is disease—and therewith cure—a conceivability. As well to a thing divine as to a purely mechanical fall, disease were an unattainable capability. *Man* only can fall ill—the man whom the Buddha points out to us, the man who through and through is a combustion, an alimentation-process, with whom at every moment of his existence energy and material stand in mutual functional dependence each upon the other. Correspondingly, it is only in a process thus constituted that the fact of cure is capable of explanation.

By the term *cure* I understand the fact that a single incitation develops a reaction which no longer stands in any kind of working relationship to the original impulse, but goes on developing itself as a self-acting increase. Such a proceeding is possible neither with a purely mechanical process of compensation nor yet with a "force in itself." It is only possible there where an energy and its material stand in a relation of mutual functional dependence.

The fact also that diseases permit of being affected by the power of the mind, by thought, is possible of explanation only where an individual energy and its material stand in a relationship of mutual dependence.

All the numberless instances of the influence of the mind over the body, of the body over the mind; all our "moods" of good and ill-humour; further, the *acquisition of habits* and the physical necessity of sleep, are explicable only in the Buddha-thought.

It may be interposed:—

"We have not the least need of the Buddha in order to see that. We have long since recognized the mutual dependence of mind and body as a necessity."

Very good! But if you have really recognized that, you must also draw the conclusions unavoidably consequent upon the same, and these consist in the intellectual necessity of individual beginninglessness. If you have not understood that, then you have understood neither the Buddha, nor actuality, nor yourselves. You have not understood the truth; you only meet it, as two cross-roads meet one another and then pass on in opposite directions. Individual beginninglessness is the key-word, the guiding clue to the Buddha-thought.

And with this we come to that most important of all problems, the problem of heredity.

IX

BUDDHISM AND THE PROBLEM OF BIOLOGY

To the question, "Whence have I sprung?" faith answers, "From God," while science answers, "From your parents." Faith calls men the children of their Father in heaven; science calls them the children of their begetter.

Meanwhile this discrepancy means no more than that the answer of science, couched in such a form, despite its apparent accuracy yields men no satisfaction. For that I am descended from my parents, on this no rational being can cast a doubt; and if the believer says that beings have sprung from God, he can only mean this in some particular respect.

Upon what foundation rests the necessity for this peculiar interpretation of facts patent to all eyes—the facts concerned with procreation?

All things in the world may be divided up into two great classes—things that admit of being generalized, and things that do not admit of being generalized. Of these, the former alone lie within reach of science, for science comes into play only where comparison and repetition are possible, comparison being a generalization in regard to what is presented simultaneously, and repetition a generalization in respect of what is presented in succession. Living beings do not admit of being either compared or repeated, hence cannot become a subject of science.

In one particular regard, it is true, living beings may be conceived of as open to comparison and repetition; but this, as pointed out, has to do only with that in the individual which precisely in a certain specific elaboration can be rendered capable of comparison and repetition—namely, that in me which is re-actual, not the actual, not that which says, "*I* am."[1] As this latter I can neither be compared nor repeated. As a being endowed with consciousness, I am a something unique, a unity—more correctly, a non-duality; and here is to be found the reason why the answer given by science never satisfies and never can satisfy. Heredity requires the single-branched tracing back of one being to another. I bestow no theory of heredity upon a flame when, on the one hand, I trace it back to the kindling wood, and on the other to the oxygen of the atmosphere. The answer of science, however, would have me, the unity, arise out of two other unities, father and mother, each of whom in their turn would spring from two other unities, and so on in geometrical progression; thus, in place of a single-branched tracing back, one infinite in its ramifications. Hence the answer of science is lacking in that which it is bound to supply if it is

[1] When a modern writer, like T. Loeb in his *Dynamik der Lebenserscheinungen*, declares living beings to be machines "which consist *essentially* of colloidal matter possessing the property of automatic alimentation and reproduction," the statement has about as much value as if one should think to explain the arc-light as something that consists *essentially* of a stick of carbon possessing the property of automatically lighting itself every evening and burning throughout the night.

to satisfy the thinker. As a something unique I am a something singly determined. If, however, I were nothing but the product of the union of an ovum-cell and a sperm-cell, there would positively be nothing present to make it necessary that precisely *I* should spring from this ovum-cell and this sperm-cell. I could just as well have sprung from the cell material out of which, as a matter of fact, my brother has come forth; while he, on his part, could just as well have come from the cell material from which in the actual event I have come. The uniquely determined goes by the board. But that that which "*I*" now am, might just as well have been some other *I*,—such an idea is a self-evident absurdity. It is not the cell matter alone that does make up the "*I*." The cell matter is only so much working material of a particular kind, and a something uniquely determining this material must appear on the scene, otherwise there would offer no possibility whatever of the fact, "*I*." To think to explain me by the cell matter alone were somewhat the same as thinking to explain the flame by the kindling wood and the oxygen of the atmosphere, exclusively.

Of such an *Hebraic* conception of the matter—to speak like Humboldt—no physicist would ever be guilty; but the biologist is. The manner in which he deals with the problem of heredity is Hebraic in the fullest sense of the word, and so fashioned that it cannot help but tumble to the ground simply of its own weight. Assuming beforehand the identity of "life" and "cell," endeavour is made to solve the riddle of life by means of description alone, the way leading from the material of generation to the new living being plotted out with ever increasing exactitude until finally an apparently uninterrupted succession stands before us; where, to be sure, it is conveniently forgotten that its seeming continuity is solely due to the fineness, the delicacy, of the isolated momentary images. As little as I can fabricate actual, living movement out of a series of stereoscopic pictures, though making never so slight the duration of each separate picture, just as little is the process of generation to be comprehended by mere description, even though it bring before us a simply endless number of phases of development. Still, I can lull myself with the delusion that by this method I am drawing ever nearer to my goal, and that salvation lies simply in the fineness of the lenses, the delicacy and ingenuity of the modes of colouring, and in patience. But far other powers than these are required for the solving of the riddle of life. For upon this line of inquiry one remains ever and always concerned with reactions. Let the discoveries thus made, the new demonstrations of the entire process supplied, be never so novel, never so interesting, withal they remain reactions, and tell us nothing save that energies *must* be present; never a word do they say bearing on these latter themselves.

This is not the place to go more closely into the details which physiology and embryology have brought to the light of day in the course of their increasingly accurate demonstration of the germination process. It must suffice to point out that all these results without exception have to do with reactions, and say nothing—absolutely nothing—

about the *essential nature* of what takes place—a fact which sufficiently indicates the extent of their value. The question as to how it is possible that a man, a living being, can be developed out of a cell, is one that is never even broached upon this line of inquiry. The question as to *actual energies* is here set aside unintentionally, as in the mechanical world-theory of the physicist it is excluded deliberately.

The reading which the Buddha-thought supplies on this question already, in what has gone before,[1] has been sufficiently worked out, and so need only be briefly summarized here. It runs as follows:—

The whole insoluble problem of heredity only arises, as with the problem of the effecting of contact and the problem of nutrition, through working with fixed quantities, with identities. As in physics one asks, "How can two bodies come into contact?" thus putting a question the answering of which is already estopped with the simple putting of the question, since in the physical sense there are no such things as "bodies"; and as in physiology one does the like when one asks, "How can the living being assimilate nutriment into itself?" where there is not anything at all present of such sort that it can assimilate something *to itself*; so in the matter of procreation the question is asked, "How is it possible that out of two biological identities a new identity can arise?" But it is not an identity at all that rises new in procreation; that truly would mean carrying out the arithmetical sum *one plus one equals one* into actual practice. Nothing happens save that material of a peculiar character, for a

[1] Cf. Essay V., "The Teaching of Kamma."

longer or shorter period, is subjected to a new state of strain of a peculiar character—has a fresh tendency imparted to it. And this new tendency, this impulsion it is, which, as Kamma coming from a previous existence, now takes hold. It takes hold where it does take hold, just because it *must* take hold there; because this location answers to it, the individual, the unique, as the only one in the universe; and all it does here is merely to stimulate, to develop that which already lies prefigured in the material, extending even to what is most singular, most individual. Were the material nothing individual, certainly no individual energy could take hold of it. But just because there is an *individual* material, therefore does it call for *individual* energy. Because the energy is *individual*, therefore does it call for *individual* material, and nowhere else can it take hold save just there where it does.

The question as to how it is possible that I can see, hear, smell, taste, feel, think, take nourishment, and so forth, here rolls back into beginninglessness, into a double question—that concerning the succession of Kamma, representing endlessness in time; and that concerning the material, representing the corresponding endlessness in space. I learn to see, hear, think, and so forth, as the flame learns to burn. Had I to learn this in the vulgar sense of the word, never in life could I compass it. As pure process of alimentation I *have* not all these powers; I *am* this potency itself. I do not *have* functions; I *am* functioning itself, as a genuine, self-acting process which burns in virtue of a genuine energy that never can *be demonstrated*, that only *demonstrates itself* in consciousness.

When *science* teaches that I am descended wholly and entirely from my parents, it teaches that the *I*-process is not kindled at all, but propels itself hither from parents, grandparents, and so forth—does not burn, but rolls—so making necessary the question as to the first beginning of this motion; for everything set in motion, urged onward—in short, every reaction—must have a first moment of beginning.

In contradistinction to science, *faith* teaches that the parents provide the material, while God sets all alight by endowing me with an immortal soul—an idea, indeed, demanding faith.

The Buddha teaches: The parents provide the material, the groundwork, and the *I*-energy of some disintegrating *I*-process corresponding uniquely to these potentialities, sets all alight. Here I take rise in my parents as the fountain takes its rise in the hill. That the fountain does so, is beyond all cavil, is patent to any eye; yet it is but as an alien guest.

Thus of the three, the Buddha is the only one to abide by actuality, the only one with whom the entire miracle of propagation takes its place among mundane events, conforming likewise to the laws of mundane occurrences. For faith, the miracle of propagation lies outside the jurisdiction of these latter; for science, it is true it remains within their jurisdiction, but only as a barren possibility.

It is here where the true thinker must clutch and claw his way in, that I would confront him, as the highwayman the traveller, with a "Sta viator!" For the simple fact that I am here, a single moment of the "*I*," yields the entire cosmogony of the Buddha. Every *I*-moment is possible, is thinkable, only as the point of intersection of the lines of Kamma and of the material, hence as the form of a world that *has* not law but itself *is* law. I am here, means, I am here as self-conscious. I am here as self-conscious, means, I am determined as one and single. I am determined as one and single, means, The twofold material of generation must be made one through some energy. That, however, means, I am without beginning.

Of what service is this idea as a working hypothesis?

The answer is: It alone makes possible a reading of the fact, "*consciousness*"—that is to say, a reading of myself which, as already shown, can never be of an inductive, but only of an intuitive nature. That which in the mode of apprehending it peculiar to science, invests the problem of heredity with a specific gravity such that of itself it must necessarily tumble to the ground, is the fact that in this apprehension of the problem consciousness falls to be included as part of that which is to furnish the demonstration.

From the standpoint physiology adopts, consciousness must reside in the groundwork, in the cell material; so that now it is a question of carrying the demonstration right on into this groundwork.

As their trump card against the materialistic and mechanistic wing of science, the idealistic and teleological wing play this: "Consciousness, thought, psychic faculty, or whatever else one chooses to name it, does not admit of being explained under the image of a motion, thus cannot be explained mechanically." And materialism yields the point with a grinding of the teeth behind which is concealed a sort of inward satisfaction that would say something to this effect: "It is quite true what you say there. We can account for everything, only not for this last little remainder, consciousness. The extent of our knowledge is best shown by this our helplessness; but the day will yet come when this holy Ilion also, this stronghold of nature and her secrets—consciousness—shall fall before our giant strokes."

With the adoption of such an attitude, science finds herself in the difficult position of having to account for consciousness from its antecedent conditions. These antecedent conditions may be followed up along two lines of inquiry; on the one hand, along the line of anatomical, physiological conditions, sense organs and brain; and on the other hand, along the line of functional conditions, of the perceptions in their varying degrees and qualities—two tasks which physiology and psychology share between them.

To the former task it is that we are indebted for the existence of one of the most splendid departments—perhaps, indeed, the most splendid department—of the physiological sciences: the physiology of the sense-organs. One may say that this line of research reveals most impressively of all the splendid poverty of science—a dazzling altogether astounding wealth of the most interesting details, which, however, instead of converging to draw nearer to the sought-for goal, lose themselves in the boundless.

That which the physiology of the sense-organs aims at is to make functioning—with what one might call suggestive violence—follow as a logical necessity from the anatomical and physiological details. The delicate intricacies of the retina, of the cortical organ, of the papillæ of smell and taste, have been laid bare with such a completeness that it seems to need but one more breath, the last and lightest of all, to wake in this wondrous instrument the melody of life. But it is just this last lightest breath that remains lacking, and is not to be secured by any mere dexterity in method however highly developed. Set to where one will, whether at the first turning over of the ovum, whether upon the heights of the evolution of sense, everywhere the miracle stands before us complete. It is entirely owing to the vast numbers and continuous relays of workers in the realm of science that the conviction that upon this path, a description becoming ever more minute and exact, there is nothing real to be achieved has not already gained much more ground than is the case. As oft as pen and scalpel fall from a trembling hand, into the breach leaps youthful vigour, and begins the battle anew with fresh courage.

The like holds good of the latest branch of psychology, the working out of prerequisite conditions of function. On all hands a similar scene meets the eye. Each new result, each fresh-won eminence avails nothing but to open out in yet more impressive fashion the vista of endless, towering mountains beyond. Here it would almost seem as if men intentionally slurred over the patent fact that the explanation of consciousness, of the power to think, already in every case presupposes this itself, and that every sensation, if at all present as such, already possesses also a certain content of consciousness. It is the chase after the horizon,—the attempt by a vigorous and decided advance to see over on the other side of one's own limit of vision,—perpetual progression without progress!

The best illustration of this is furnished by what I might call the naïve disunion prevailing within psychology's own camp. The various movements are not infrequently to be found fighting against one another, like different divisions of the same army in the darkness of night. One party says: "In the analysis of the sensations lies all our salvation. Out of them only can we have consciousness arise synthetically, and, all said and done, up to our time science has achieved nothing just because she has neglected this natural prerequisite to all possibilities of knowledge." The which, it may be remarked in passing, is somewhat cold comfort after more than two thousand years of labour! Then suddenly a counter-movement interjects: "The sensations are what one may not seek to analyse."[1] Well, that is what I should call plagiarizing the words of the *bon dieu* in the Garden of Eden: "Of the tree of knowledge thou shalt not eat." If I may not lay finger upon the fount of my existence, what boots to me the never so broad but turbid stream of the lower levels?

If one compares with this utter lack of success the indubitable honesty of the effort, the entire phenomenon "science" assumes something of an air of sublime absurdity, of melancholy enthusiasm, such as ever and again recalls to one's mind the immortal hero of Cervantes' romance—vigorous, single-hearted effort from a mistaken standpoint, directed towards a mistaken end.

As a matter of fact, however, in these latter days the impossibility of the old path with reference to

[1] E. Mach, *Erkenntnis und Irrtum.*

the problem of consciousness seems to be perceived. But the new path upon which in their need men have entered is an utterly paradoxical one; it is the modern theory of the cell endowed with consciousness in the shape of the faculty of memory. Seeing no possibility whatever of explaining consciousness into the cell material without more ado they have recourse to the device of making the cell set out on its campaign, so to speak, with the faculty of memory in its knapsack.[1] In this manner they rid themselves once for all of the mischief-maker, "consciousness"; and with astounding simplicity change ground to a position whence they can fight out the battle about a world-theory after the fashion of army manœuvres, all according to programme

[1] Thus, Hering writes in *Das Gedächtniss als Funktion der belebten Materie*: "The central sections of the nervous system must retain some memory of that which they formerly have done. . . . In like manner the motor system must possess memory, albeit unknown to us it is true." Further on he says: "The reappearance in the daughter organism of the characteristics of the mother organism is a reproduction on the matter side, of such a process as the former already once before has shared in, if only as germ in the ovary, which process it remembers, inasmuch as to like stimuli it reacts exactly as that organism of which it once formed a part"; from which the fact of the hereditary transmission of characteristic qualities would work out as a specimen merely of the "memory of unconscious matter." Hering adds: "Thus every organic being of the present day stands before us ultimately as a product of the unconscious memory of organized matter."

All such ideas are nothing but ingenious paraphrases of actuality; and in the last analysis amount to nothing but an audacious juggle with the word *memory*. And when it is further said: "If memory be attributed to the species the same as to the individual, instinct immediately becomes comprehensible"; and in conclusion: "The conscious memory of man is extinguished at death, but the unconscious memory of nature is indestructible," I can only call this dealing in poetry, not science, a possibility only to be arrived at by the *dis*-actualizing of actuality. In reality memory exists solely where something is remembered, just as a flame exists there only where it is burning. Of this kind of memory, however, but one example is to be found in all the world—I myself! It is just this lack of the sense of actuality—as displayed in physics—which to such a large extent constitutes the greatness of science, while it also no less constitutes its weakness, as in biology. E. Mach in his *Erkenntnis und Irrtum*, p. 49, expresses himself to the self-same effect: "Heredity, instinct, may then be depicted as memory stretching out beyond the individual," a sentence that possesses about as much content of actuality as the "songs unsung" of a dead poet.

upon any lines that may be desired. "Give me a chaos and out of it I will make you a world," says Kant in his *Prolegomena*. "Give me a cell and out of it I will make you a Goethe or a Newton," says the modern biologist. The necessary arrangements are all made, the "stern wrestle with the problems of life" can begin in the shape of fantasies drawn from the *Ratskeller* of the Alma Mater. If one hews out the building stones to one's own fancy, one may indeed erect systems—a mechanics, a thermo-dynamics, but never a genuine world-conception.

The possibility of ideas such as these is to be found in what I might call the mechanizing of biological values. Thinking is represented, along with heat, as a molecular vibration; the psychic act, under the figure of an impress, of an "Engramm,"[1] thus of work accomplished; and therewith we get the possibility of that rolling back of the *I*-process from the individual to his begetters, and from these in turn to their begetters, and so on backwards *ad infinitum*—in short, the possibility of remaining upon the lines of the purely material, which partakes of the nature of a reaction precisely as much as the lines upon which the physicist works in the cosmogony peculiar to energetics. Just as there, from the outset, the real energies are left out of consideration and only their reactions dealt with, looked upon as work done; so in the treatment of the problem of heredity by science the whole process of life is looked upon simply as work done, in biological guise, a mode of apprehending it to which scientific thought itself, as re-

[1] Cf. R. Semon, *Die Mneme*.

presented by the teleological school, is entirely opposed.[1]

With the mechanistic representation of things is necessarily involved the question as to the seat of consciousness. Modern physiology vaunts itself not a little upon having got beyond the follies of the centuries that are past, when this seat was sought for in all sorts of hidden nooks. But sooth to say, its own position nowise differs; the change is only in the means of defence employed. Now, as formerly, endeavour is made to localize consciousness in certain regions; there is a search for the "seat" of consciousness. Whether as a pure hypothesis I transfer this seat to the pineal gland, or whether, from the results of experiments upon animals, I seek by a process of exclusion, as it were, to find it in the cerebral cortex—all this makes no essential difference. The mistake, the Hebraism, lies in seeking for a "seat" of consciousness at all. To such an idea only a few exceptionally clear minds oppose a front of resistance. As an example, I cite in a footnote a passage from E. Mach's *Analyse der Empfindungen*.[2]

1 "They (the materialists) teach that in the central nervous system also all is only the oscillation of atoms, only reflex motion, only mechanics. In one part of the brain only, there in the grey substance of a portion of the cerebral cortex, something takes place which as yet we are unable to explain. But it is only a question of time. Sooner or later it will certainly be demonstrated that this also is nothing but mechanics, nothing more than a complicated species of reflex action" (Bunge, *Physiologie*, i. p. 164).

2 "The practice of treating the unanalysed *I*-complex as an indivisible unity frequently finds scientific expression in singular fashion. First of all, the nervous system is set apart from the body as being the seat of sensation. In the nervous system, again, the brain is picked out as likeliest to be such a seat. And, finally, in order to save the supposed psychic unity, search is made in the brain for a *point* as the seat of the soul. Views so crude as these, however, are but ill adapted to indicate beforehand even in roughest outline the path of future investigation as to the connection between the physical and the psychical." Comparison should also be made with the introductory remarks to the chapter on "Der Sitz des Bewusstseins" in Bunge's *Physiologie*.

Singular reflections are provoked when one contrasts with these extravagant profundities the conception of things presented by the Indian thinker six hundred years before the Christian era began. In the Buddha-thought there is no something called "consciousness," as equally there is no something called "life." There is only an experience of the unfolding of consciousness—a constant *becoming conscious.* I do not *have* consciousness as I might have a half-crown in my pocket, but I *am* consciousness objectified, as I am will objectified. As long as I think in terms of actuality, there is just but *one* consciousness in the world—I myself. As long as I think in terms of actuality, consciousness means just this and no more—to experience myself. But this is possible only as an intuition, and a specific impulsion, instruction, is needed in order to arrive at this intuition. Consciousness, just like all the remainder of the *I*-process, is a form of the individual process of nutrition; the only difference is this, that it is the last, the highest phase, as the fruit is the last, the highest phase of the vegetative process. To speak of a "seat" of consciousness has about as much meaning as to speak of a "seat" of bodily heat. All this falls under the one inclusive concept, "nutrition." What modern physicist would ever be so childish as in some hot body to search for the "seat" of heat? But physiologist and biologist stagger along exhausted under the load of their learnedness on the subject of the "seat" of consciousness. There is just as much reason, and no more, for holding the brain-cells of the cerebral cortex to be the seat of consciousness as there is for regarding the electric cells in its central telegraph office as the seat of the intelligence of a great city.

The teaching of Buddhist physiology is as follows :—

Where the eye and forms encounter one another, and the antecedent conditions are such that each acts upon the other, there arises visual consciousness. Where the ear and sounds encounter one another, there arises aural consciousness. Where nose and odours encounter one another, there arises olfactory consciousness. Where tongue and flavours encounter one another, there arises gustatory consciousness. Where bodies and objects come in contact with one another, there arises tactile consciousness. Where thinking and things (known abstractly) encounter one another, there arises thought-consciousness.

"If the inward eye is undamaged, and external objects do not come within the range of vision, and (as a consequence) no corresponding interaction takes place, then a corresponding moment of consciousness does not result. If the inward eye is undamaged, and external objects come within the range of vision, and (nevertheless) no corresponding interaction takes place, then also a corresponding moment of consciousness does not result. If, however, the inward eye is undamaged, and external objects come within the range of vision, and the corresponding interaction takes place, then there results the corresponding moment of consciousness."[1]

Thus my entire individuality, the totality of individual experience is a *becoming conscious* at every

[1] *Majjhima Nikāya*, Sutta 28.

moment of existence. Consciousness is a Sankhāra, like all else, distinguished therefrom only in this, that in it Kamma itself becomes perceptible to sense.

Were teleology and mechanistics to come before the Buddha and say, "Decide thou! Which of us two is right? Is the eye born of seeing, or is seeing born of the eye? Is the brain born of thinking, or is thinking born of the brain?" the Buddha would reply with a smile:—

"My young friends, you are both right because you are both wrong. Your question is not correctly put. There are no such things as 'eye' and 'brain' in the sense in which you use the words. There is only an *I*-process, that unfolds itself by way of certain differentiations which in themselves run their course at a pace sufficiently slow to justify such separate verbal designations as the 'eye,' the 'brain,' and so forth. Your question, 'Is the eye born of seeing, or is seeing born of the eye? Is the brain born of thinking, or is thinking born of the brain?' would have sense and meaning only if the eye and the brain were in themselves organs all finished and complete, to which in that case a specific function also would have to correspond. All this, however, is nothing but a phase, nothing but the form of development assumed by a single process. It is not the eye that sees: *you* see. The eye is neither born of seeing, nor yet is seeing born of the eye; the eye is simply *the form under which seeing exists.* You do not see *with* the eye but in virtue of the fact of eye-evolution, the same as you think in virtue of the fact of brain-evolution, which is only another way of saying that you are the form assumed by individual energies."

Here the physiologist breaks in: "That consciousness has its seat in certain regions of the cerebral cortex may be proven by experiments on animals." But this is a conclusion as grossly mistaken as that of the physicist when he imagines he can follow up energy throughout all its ramifications.[1] What can be got at by experimental methods is merely negative phenomena, and these furnish no warrant for coming to conclusions as to the seat of consciousness. If I cut through the wire connected with an electric light at any point at all in the circuit, the negative phenomenon "darkness" assuredly supervenes; but to say on that account, "The point of section must be the seat of the electric energy; here is ocular demonstration," would be sheer foolishness. Yet the physiologist is guilty of just such foolishness, and at its behest does not stick at the perpetration of all those cruelties such as are scarcely to be avoided in experiments upon animals. If only the time would come when true ideas about life would take possession of science, the laboratories of physiologists would no longer be those places where every day sacrifice is made to error as in the temples of blood-stained idols.

All these researches on the subject of the seat of consciousness are only possible where one is working with empty concepts. If one thinks in terms of actuality consciousness is just that with regard to which a reading, a working hypothesis of an inductive nature, is utterly impossible; for here the reading is precisely the form assumed by the consciousness, by that which is to do the reading,

[1] Cf. Essay VII.

by the problem itself, and thus itself again requires a reading, and so on *ad infinitum*.

But there is another point involved in this problem of "consciousness" which, so far as I know, has never been taken account of, and yet is of the utmost significance.

As the Darwinian idea does not embrace in its purview the case of hybrid formations—it does not react upon it at all—so the scientific mode of envisaging things does not take in the case of the physiological negative phenomena of consciousness, does not at all react upon it. With the apparatus of science there is no possibility whatever of getting at such facts as "faith," "illusion," "error," "forgetting." Science requires something sensible and objective, something so constituted that I can rank it along with other things. In no respect, however, are any of these negative phenomena objective things. Here no possible point of entry offers for science with its instrument, induction.

I may indeed *read* consciousness under the figure of associative occurrences, but only in the form of recollection. Applied to the corresponding dissociative event, forgetting, this explanation is as impossible as that a molecular mixture which has once come to equilibrium within itself should again spontaneously return to dissolution, to dissociation. As the natural adjustment of differences of molecular tension may be explained or read as a fall, so in its associative activities consciousness may be explained or read as a fall, but never so in its dissociative activities. This, however, involves the utter worthlessness of the former explanation; for every mixture, every association, presupposes separation, dissociation, and, called upon to indicate the *essence* of consciousness, what I should point to is not so much the associative as the dissociative, not so much recollection, conjunction, as forgetting, disjunction. Once the stone is raised from the earth's surface its return fall forthwith ensues. But it is the separation from the earth's surface for which effective causes must be found. In like manner, it is dissociation, forgetting, that really demands elucidation; association, recollection can as easily be read mechanistically as the fall of a stone once it has been raised. Dissociation is the physiological miracle, in presence of which science stands altogether helpless.

The like holds good of faith, illusion, error. The purely mechanistic conception of things, the view which regards the *I*-process simply as an instance of the phenomenon of the compensation of tensile differences, can never be accommodated to the possibility of such things as faith, illusion, and error. But a similar impossibility also exists for the teleological apprehension of the world. How should a "force" ever acquire the faculty of deceiving itself or of falling into error? To a compensation-phenomenon pure and simple, as to God, illusion and error are wholly unattainable potentialities; they belong to mankind alone, to the man whom the Buddha points out to us.

If I am nothing but an unceasing reaction to the outer world, if I constantly adapt myself to things and things adapt themselves to me, not as a mere adjustment but in virtue of specific energies, only then are faith, illusion, error, and all other negative phenomena equally possible with all positive phenomena. Beginningless process furnishes the possibility of both.

Such things as actual illusion, actual error, science may nowise recognize, for in so doing she would be recognizing something for which there is absolutely no room in her cosmogony. One would thereby introduce functions for which one could furnish no organized basis. Only in the cosmogony of the Buddha, only in the concept of individual beginninglessness does each find its necessary place. Here they are the necessary preconditions of all existence. Science is powerless to defend herself against them otherwise than by an attempt to "explain away" such occurrences out of the order of world-events. Upon this point E. Mach, in his *Analyse der Empfindungen*, expresses himself as follows: "The phrase, 'illusion of the senses,' shows that man has not yet rightly come to a consciousness, or at least has not yet found it necessary to express such consciousness in fitting terminology, that the senses indicate neither false nor true. The only 'true' of which one can speak in connection with the sense organs is that under different conditions they yield different sensations and perceptions. Since these conditions are so extremely manifold in their variety . . . it may very well seem . . . as if the organ acts dissimilarly under similar conditions. Results out of the usual order are what men are accustomed to call illusions." This is to make illusion merely truth in an infinitesimal form, to "read" it as a special form of truth, and so be rid of it.

But the value of the Buddha-thought in this domain does not end here. Over and above, it explains to begin with, the every-day fact of experience, that not every pairing evolves a new embryo. This fact is alike incapable of explanation whether from the standpoint of faith or from that of science.

Faith, which sees a divine soul breathed into the material of generation, permits of no standpoint at all, since for it everything takes place according to God's good pleasure. From the standpoint of science, however, with every conjunction of ovum and sperm-cell, conception also must be granted, since here both are already the form of the new life, already contain in themselves all the ingredients of this new life. It is only the Buddha-thought that explains why, meanwhile, despite the union of ovum and sperm, conception does not take place: it has not "struck in." At the moment when both were open to the inflow of the energy, the latter was not ready. In the ceaseless, unbroken attunement, each to the other, of the happenings of a world, the proper moment was let slip.[1]

The Buddha-thought further explains the else inexplicable fact of the simultaneous resemblance and lack of resemblance between parents and children. The view of the matter taken by faith supplies no argument in favour of any kind of resemblance whatever between the two. The soul is inbreathed by God whithersoever it pleaseth him. In the view of science, on the contrary, there is found no argument for any failure in resemblance betwixt progenitors and offspring. Ever and always the characteristics of the latter can only be a combination of the characteristics of both the parents. In the Buddha-thought *alone* are similarity and dissimilarity alike accounted for. I may have inherited my father's

[1] Cf. Essay V., the citation from the *Majjhima Nikāya*, Sutta 38.

nose, his manner of blowing it indeed, since all lay foreshadowed in the material, and was obliged so to evolve itself: but the evolver is a stranger, hence one common starting-point yields an independent evolving series. Here conception means no more than that two paths, two lines, that of the material and that of energy, intersect one another. We are as at some cross-road, where two highways meet, only to lead further and further away from each other the further we pursue them.

The third item that finds an explanation in the Buddha-thought is the fact of innate aptitudes. Where the act of learning is envisaged from a purely empirical point of view these are a standing, incomprehensible miracle. Opposed to this, the defectiveness of the nativistic theory resides in the fact that according to it every being must make his appearance fitted out all complete with fixed, inborn abilities. Midway removed from both extremes stands the Buddha. With equal ease he explains the possibility of gradual development and that of appearance all ready and complete, inasmuch as with him all depends upon the *tempo* at which the energy closing with the material enters upon its unfolding process. Is the *tempo* so fast that the organic recipients are already developed upon leaving the womb, then the innate abilities are there present; the organs can set to forthwith, the external world acts immediately as liberating lure, and the nativists have the last word. Is the *tempo* slow, then there set in processes that admit of being empirically interpreted or read as a gradual attainment of faculty by experience.

Apart, however, from the biological facts, the

Buddha-thought also explains those lofty speculations that have haunted the minds of men from the earliest times, such as "previous existence," Plato's idea of learning as "reminiscence," and so forth. "Many a time it has seemed to me as if I must have been in existence once already," says such a clear, keen mind as Lichtenberg. Indeed here, if one likes, even the Kantian "*a priori* of all experience," this pure *ens* of scholasticism, acquires sense and meaning. That which with Kant stands out from reality as a blind end, destitute of any real foothold, like the spirit moving upon the face of the waters, here balls itself together into the *I myself*. My Kamma is the "*a priori*"; in a sense, such as Kant never suspected, it is true. All these minds lack guidance, lack light. In dim fashion they feel, but they do not see. During my latest sojourn at Anuradhapura, in the course of a conversation with the abbot of Ruanwelli, he said to me, "Every one who is without the Teaching is like the blind elephant in the jungle: he feels at every twig"—to find out if it is eatable. Here we have an apt illustration of inquiring ignorance.

With this solution of the problem of procreation as furnished by the Buddha are involved a few necessary questions which might have been disposed of in our fifth essay, but may more fitly be dealt with here.

The first is this:—

"If, as said above, the uniquely appropriate energy is not always ready for the material, if contact can be missed, must then a quota of material always stand ready for the Kamma that is set free at every death?"

To which the answer is: "That a faggot should miss the kindling spark; this may very well happen, but that the kindling spark should find nothing upon which to act, such is never the case." Its very being is just its taking hold, the actuity itself. The *I*-energy takes hold there precisely where it can take hold.

But will it always take hold just there where legitimately it ought to take hold? Will it take hold rightly?

To put such a question is the same as if one should ask: "Will the sun indicate mid-day correctly and unfailingly every day? Or: Will the ocean maintain itself unceasingly at sea-level?" Where the entire universe *has* not but *is* law there, "to take hold" is as much as to say "to take hold legitimately": "to take hold legitimately" is as much as to say "to take hold rightly." All such questions were justified only if we had to do with a reciprocal being attuned; but all things are found to be a series of ever new self-attunings, each after other—no working into one another like cog and groove, no pre-established harmony, no psycho-physical parallelism. The whole universe is a thing that finds itself in a state of perpetual nascency. If a jest may be ventured in face of the monster, one might say that the whole world is constantly in a state of bringing forth, yet never is there born a "something" that stands ideally fast, so as to be fitted to serve as a standard for true and untrue.

The fact that a chemical compound decomposes, that its constituent elements are set free, always implies that from another direction forces more powerful are coming into play. Decomposition is nothing but the form of a new combination. In similar wise Kamma does not become free just for the sake of becoming free, just in order to be free. Not in any arbitrary fashion does it leap out of its old location; it does so only because its material falls away from under it. That it can take fresh hold and always can take hold, of this the guarantee is the simple fact that there is a world at all, for the latter is just the series of self-attunings each after other, itself. Were the world obliged to *come* to this self-attuning first, never by any means could there be a world. What we find present is precisely something given—actuality, and this stands for no mere set of *possibilities*; it represents a *power*—its own power to exist; and the expression of this power to exist is just this eternal ability to take fresh hold.

To change the simile: For every falling stone there is always ready the spot on which it can fall. For along with the fact "falling stone" are also given all the pre-requisite conditions in which such questions as, "Where can it fall? Will it find its spot?" are already met and answered. Its fall is nothing motiveless; it does not fall blindly, by pure accident. Neither is its fall any previously determined affair; it does not fall towards any given goal. Its fall is an attuning of itself, an accommodating of itself to its goal. In the act of falling it finds its goal. In the same way this my whole existence is simply my finding my way, my accommodating of myself to the new goal. Kamma does not *go* to its new place as a spontaneous force, nor does it *fall*, as a mere reaction, but it advances itself as a flame advances itself. In the beginningless happenings of a world, living at every moment accommodates itself to living. It is like a universal round dance, this Samsāra. Kamma has seized his partner, and with her whirls through the infinitudes until she collapses with fatigue, is worn out, or, become clumsy and heavy, slips from him because she no longer suits him. She no longer suits him, however, because there is another whom she suits better. Thus does the material pass from hand to hand, because one lender snatches it away from the other.

> Indeed 'twas only borrowed—the lenders are so many!

And thus is disposed of that other question: "Once set alight, could not an *I*-process burn for ever?"

Science, because it never can be actual science, makes an effort at least not to be of the laity, and endeavours to make good this its distinctive characteristic by the striking, one might almost say the sensational, manner in which it formulates its problems. Thus it tries to signalize the commanding nature of its standpoint with respect to the problems of life by telling the dumbfounded layman of a death that is purely a phenomenon of adaptation—yea more, of a death that is nothing but a bad habit. Upon this point, Weismann in his *Dauer des Lebens* says: "From a purely physiological standpoint there is no perceivable reason why it should not be possible for the fission of the cells to proceed *ad infinitum, i.e.* for the organism to function eternally. To me the necessity for death is intelligible only from the standpoint of utility. . . . An individual that lived for ever would always become infirm and useless to the species. Death is merely a utilitarian arrangement; it is no necessity, grounded in the essential nature of life." This is about as sensible as if one said, relying upon the facts of kitchen routine, "The going out of the fire is merely a utilitarian arrangement: it is no necessity grounded in the essential nature of fire." To speak of death as a phenomenon of adaptation is to juggle with death as with some empty concept. In truth it is not as some think, death that accommodates itself to life, but simply thinking to the facts. The crass absurdity only becomes evident when out of this mere "reading" of the facts one seeks to evolve a truth of practical application, as Metchnikoff does in his "daring" surmises. I assert that science ought to be ashamed of herself for filling the nursery room of mankind with such fabulous tales of the future, when already the air is thick enough with the fables of the past. The old Salernitanian school of medicine used to ask: "*Cur moritur homo, cui crescit salvia in hortis?*" In much the same way the new—nay, the very newest—school of medicine demands: "Why does man die, for whom in the laboratory grows the Maya Yoghurt?" thereby showing that in the depths below the surface she grows on the same stock as the so much contemned "blind faith."

Like a grown man among children stands the Buddha towards such fictions. With him death is nothing but living in a new environment. The distaff keeps ceaselessly turning; it is only that a new clump of wool has been placed on it. The discernment that life is of the nature of a process involves of necessity the discernment that life can persist only so long as the active affinities concerned are not overmastered by other affinities. Here again, to be sure, I can interpret death as a phenomenon of accommodation, but equally as well can I so interpret life, for here I am just the beginningless self-accommodating, self-attuning itself. However varied the length of time during which the attuning may last, however it may be prolonged by the use of specific contrivances, to speak of a potential immortality is to do away with the process-like nature of life, to make the never-resting actuality stiffen into a childish counterfeit. With the fact that I am born, the fact of dying is *guaranteed* me. For beings can only be born if previously they have died; they must buy themselves their birth with their own death. Were we not born, then, to be sure, we need not die either. But to be born and yet not to see in death a necessity grounded in the very nature of life, this demands place alongside that passage in the book of Joshua: "Sun, stand thou still upon Gibeon; and thou, Moon, in the valley of Ajalon." What a different ring has this word of the Master: "That that which has life should not meet with death—such a thing is not!" And yet it is so! We demand life-values at any cost; and, are the udders milked dry, then must death itself make good the lack!

If science and the Buddha-thought be placed alongside one another for mutual and unbiassed comparison, perforce the superiority of the latter must be acknowledged, since by it is neatly resolved in one single conception that which science with two distinct concepts makes an inextricable tangle of. From the point of view of science, dying is every whit as much of a miracle as being born, since in birth a new identity appears on the scene all entire, and in death all as entire vanishes; in the same way that to a child's idea a thunder-storm as such, *i.e.* taken purely as a symptom, is something that arises all entire, and all entire passes away again. The simple fact is: despite all the technical skill with which she handles the problem of heredity, and notwithstanding all the suggestions made to the understanding to recognize as uninterrupted the passage from life to life, science has her abode in the realm of the miraculous. The technique of her descriptions, to which she gives the misleading title, "doctrine of evolution," leave the actual problem of evolution entirely untouched. In face of the miracles of birth and death, science strongly resembles a boy making his first observations in natural history. Finding in his glass-case the caterpillar dead and the butterfly born, he will say, "Two miracles! The old has died and something new has made its appearance." Instead of both facts merging into one another in a true conception of what has taken place, to his mistaken notion they fall apart from one another, and become problems defying solution. Even so is it with science. Through her failure to recognize that the facts of birth here and death there are forms of one and the same experience instead of a single comprehension of both under the one aspect, two miracles are found by her to be present. The noose of life has become a knot, and every attempt to undo it by continued pulling only makes worse the tangle. On this point the physicist has already left the stage of childhood behind. To-day he no longer says, "Two miracles! Heat is gone and motion is present." He has found the clue, albeit, it is true, only in form of reaction. The biologist, however, still remains incapable of replacing two miracles with a true and genuine conception. He is still unaware that it is with dying that being born must be purchased. Hence he treats birth as a fact by itself, and death as a fact by itself, and so remains confronting both problems internally insoluble.

So much for that point. A further question that suggests itself is: "Could not a Kamma be simultaneously attuned in two or more places?"

To this the answer would be: "Theoretically, so long as one confronts the problem from the mechanistic standpoint, that is, from the standpoint that deals only with reactions, it is attuned in places innumerable." In exactly the same way a drop of water, as it trickles downward, theoretically can have innumerable points as its resting-place; practically, however, it will have one single resting-place, and this latter will prove itself the resting-place and the one single resting-place among countless possibilities simply and solely by the fact that the drop comes to a halt just at this spot. Actuality is simple as singly determined. It only becomes complex in the mechanistic mode of apprehending it; that is, where reactions alone are dealt with.

Again, it may be asked: "Could not two Kammas attune themselves to one and the same body of material?"

But this question has just as much meaning as if one asked, "Could not two men appropriate to themselves, assimilate, and be nourished by, the same loaf of bread?" So long as one treats of "bread" in purely theoretical fashion, eats concepts, well and good! But if one eats in actuality, the absurdity becomes obvious.

Again: "Might it not happen for once that the ovum should conduct the lightning without the assistance of the sperm-cell?"

So far as mankind is concerned, the only reply is that here both factors are required. It simply is so! Why are certain reactions brought about only when certain catalytic agents or ferments are introduced? How weighty the above objection has always been to the mind of mankind is shown by the important rôle which "immaculate conception" has played from the earliest times. That in itself it is not impossible the animal kingdom sufficiently attests. With man, however, the conditions are so disposed that both, ovum- and sperm-cell, are required in order to conduct the Kamma and cause it to take hold.

If one asks: "But could not this also happen outside a maternal womb?" I reply: "I do not know." It certainly does not happen with man. It happens with cold-blooded creatures, with dogs, and so forth. In the botanical gardens at Peradeniya, Ceylon, in the climate the most perfect in the world for vegetation, there are several trees—the *Bertholetia excelsa* of Brazil, for example—which, despite the similarity of the climate to that of their native haunts, as yet have resisted all attempts to propagate them. It simply is so! Actuality lays down its own laws because it is itself law. Science can do nothing but hobble along as best she may in the wake of all these facts, and endeavour to accommodate herself to them. But what bears witness in favour of the Buddha-thought is precisely the impossibility of getting fecundation to take place outside a womb, or of bringing it about by introducing sperm into the uterus by artificial means, of which latter proceeding a single, not altogether unequivocal instance is reported by an American gynæcologist. What is needed is the living energy which for a limited period vibrates in the material like the energy in the plucked string of a lute. It is just this vibrating energy in it which first makes the material to be material, *i.e.* the thing that is capable of a unique attunement.

And here we come to the most important question of all :—

" Is a human Kamma always obliged to take fresh hold precisely of human *I*-material? Would it not be possible for once, that human Kamma should be attuned to animal material or reverse wise, animal Kamma to human material?" To this the answer is : Kamma can take hold only where there is material that itself is the form of a Kamma. How far down in the kingdom of living creatures this material extends cannot be said any more than in the case of a flame can be indicated exactly how far the circle of its radiance extends, the precise limit stated at which it gives place to darkness. And just as, despite this, the flame has a definite circle of radiance, so Kamma has a definite sphere of operation, albeit no science—such as zoology or anthropology and so forth—is in a position to establish this thesis. Kamma takes hold where it can take hold—that is to say, where in the material of procreation there vibrate energies to which it is uniquely attuned; and in the scale of living creatures it reaches just as far as it is able to reach.

In the Jatakas, the birth-stories of the Buddha, we see him in Samsāra ranging this whole scale through from the lowest stages of the animal kingdom right up to the worlds of the gods, ever and again planting foot there where the Kamma was attuned at the moment of collapse.

It is a fact of experience that between living beings there exist peculiar consonances. To a stone or a tree no tie of compassion binds us. Compassion only begins at the animal world, and its limits are individual, and vary according to bringing up. With many compassion is entirely confined to human beings; more especially is this the case with those brought up in the shadow of monotheistic beliefs. In pantheism, on the contrary, as it has prevailed in India from the earliest days, the boundary line of compassion runs right down into the lowest animal kingdom. Meanwhile, among us, too, those incapable of feeling compassion for a dog, a horse, a cow, a cage-bird, are very few.

In the last analysis the capacity for compassion consists in the peculiar attunement, consonance existing between one *I*-energy and other *I*-energies. Where, as in the case of the stone, there are no *I*-energies, there can likewise be no compassion.

In the Buddha-thought the classification of the phenomena of life adopted is one peculiar to itself alone. The usual crude divisions into stone, plant, animal, and man, or into inorganic and organic, count for nothing here. All these are based upon the assumption that things are fixed quantities, identities; hence they prescribe artificial preconditions, and consequently have no value in themselves but only with reference to some such determined end as increased facility of comprehension. In the Buddha-thought all life-phenomena divide themselves into these two classes—those that have power to act upon me, stimulate or excite me, set me in sympathetic vibration and correspondingly be set in sympathetic vibration by me, and those with which this is not more or not yet the case.

We are bound to admit—and all physiological phenomena bear witness to it—that the ovum- and sperm-cell are those forms of development of the *I*-process in which the *I*-energy of the individuals concerned reveals itself in its purest and most intimate, because most intrinsic form. If they are torn apart from the whole in the act of generation, yet are they able to furnish the new *I*-material, because they keep the *I*-energy vibrating sufficiently long in themselves to be able to answer to the Kamma peculiarly attuned to them.

Such an apprehension of things would seem like a slap in the face for biology and the whole history of evolution, and here the task of the Buddha-thought is to come to an understanding with the theory of descent if it is to prove satisfactory to the man of education.

To begin with, one must be quite clear on this point—that the whole theory of descent is nothing but a form of reading the biological facts, a theory in the strictest sense of the word. As a consequence it has value only with reference to certain ends. First, in order to group together under one main heading the enormous miscellany of facts—thus, for didactic ends. And secondly, read from below upwards instead of from above downwards, that is, apprehended as a theory of evolution instead of as a theory of descent, it suggests a life-value of such inspiring power as in this respect might also be set alongside the ideas of God and of the state—the idea of a development of mankind that progresses ever further and further. This idea, of course, is much older than Darwin, but it was only in his teaching that for the first time it assumed requisite reality.

The evolution theory is far removed from Darwin's original teaching upon natural selection and the survival of the fittest. It has only been read into it by this age of ours ever hungering after life-values. Man must have something to which to cling in the dread wastes of endlessness; he must have something that points beyond this life—something to which he can relate this life as a whole. To an age whose belief in God more and more dwindles away, the evolution theory is an invaluable substitute. Even if it yields no real nourishment, yet does it point in emblem beyond this life of the individual, and soothes like the sight of a beautiful picture. That in reality one can only speak of evolution where one has at hand a standard one can apply to it, to the progress made—in other words, where one can measure it; this men forget and willingly forget, for this single consideration perforce flings the whole idea of progressive evolution into the category of illusions. We must have an absolute point of departure if we are to speak of evolution in itself. This we no more possess than we possess an absolute space to which we can relate its motion. Where an absolute point of departure is lacking, the idea of evolution is as meaningless as the idea of absolute motion. The evolutional is "interpreted into" the facts by main force. To declare man to be more evolved than the monads, savours of a limited despotism. The directly opposite view were every whit as possible. Since the monads achieve life with an infinitely much simpler apparatus than man, they therefore stand higher in evolution; for "it is in limitation that the master is revealed." A great many animals can do very much more than man with his organ of thought, the main purpose of which, when all is said and done, would appear to consist in putting obstacles between him and actual life, and subjecting him to the tyranny of concepts. In point of fact, however, the miracle of the cells is everywhere the same, in the monads as in the brain-cells, and one position is all as futile as the other.

In the fact that science as represented by biology is particularly qualified to adopt the development-idea in the form of the theory of evolution, and to make use of it, she shows her deep-lying and essential fellowship with faith. For where in this sense there is development, there is beginning; where there is beginning, there is an absolute; and where there is an absolute, there is faith. To honest, genuine thinking, every thing, every moment of beginning, whether of a real or of a conceptual nature, leads back to a beginninglessness. In the simple existence of life, that is, of anything that is alive, its beginninglessness is already implied. With this the evolution idea is deprived of all possibility. Here development signifies nothing but the unfolding of the characteristics involved in the material laid hold of. Actual development proceeds just as much from seed to blossom as from blossom to seed. A moment of *evolution* is as little to be found in the happenings of the world as in a burning flame. To hold one world-period as more developed than another is a childish position. Every moment demonstrates, simply by its existence, that it is *the* form of adaptation which just at that moment is the only possible and therefore necessary one. The world of the cosmic nebula—as being the blossom of earlier worlds, the seed of later ones—is as developed as the world of the ichthyosaurus, as the world of the *homo sapiens*. All are forms of the series of self-attunings, each after other. To call the world of the *now* more developed than the world of the Coal Age were somewhat the same as to call the descent of a stone after it has been falling for five seconds more developed than when it has been falling for one second. The downward velocity after one second is *the* adaptation just as much as is the downward velocity after five seconds. It only shows the childishness of the biological apprehension of things that it should still continue to find satisfaction in such trivialities, based wholly as these are upon concepts of its own fabrication.

But as already said, in the original teaching of Darwin nothing is to be found of such conceptions. He was a good Christian who had not the remotest idea of setting up a primordial cell as competitor against the *bon dieu*, or of aping him with such like theories. And when he happens to meet him on his way, he humbly pulls off his hat like Hodge in presence of "squire."

The essence of Darwinism is contained in the theory of selection. Against this theory reproach has been brought that it embraces in its scope only the transformations, not the arising of living creatures. Rarely has theory encountered reproach more childish and mistaken. That is found fault with, which precisely constitutes the very greatness of the thought.

Darwin's thesis is as follows :—

"Given the existence of organic matter, given its tendencies to transmit its characteristics. Given, finally, the life conditions of the organic matter—these things in their totality are the causes of the present and past conditions of organic nature."

The greatness of this statement lies in its truly scientific exactitude, in its purely mechanistic apprehension of things. Just as the physicist, when he speaks of force and mass, intentionally eliminates everything of the actual—he simply cannot work until first all that is actual is eliminated, and pure relation-values established—so Darwin eliminates everything actual and sets to work with pure relation-values. Otherwise put: His teaching is nothing but a new system of measurement for actuality; and his greatness consists in this, that he was the first to take biology and apply to it the methods of the physicist. He it was who first approached the biological facts from the standpoint of differences of tension, differences of potentiality. His doctrine of the survival of the fittest is simply a kind of biological measure of force. What would one say of a man who made it a matter of reproach in connection with a yard-stick that it did not also at the same time indicate the nature and origin of the object measured by it? Only when it is independent of all such questions can anything serve as a standard of measurement. Where would the physicist find himself were he to say, "I will not concern myself with forces until I really know what force is?" He does not wish to know what force is. Were one to tell him he would stop his ears. He wants to make use of force, to be able to measure it; nothing more. In the same way Darwin does not in the least want to know and tell what living beings are. Should one say, "They are from God," another, "They are from the devil," he, Darwin, happens to be of the former opinion; but that has nothing to do with the problem before him. As the physicist lays hold of the pendulum in its swing and says, "If now I let it go, such and such phenomena must occur," so Darwin—figuratively speaking of course—lays hold of the biological pendulum and says, "If now I let it go, this and this must happen." The physicist so arranges his preliminary conditions that he can measure what occurs, and so also does Darwin. As the physical resultant is measured in the form of work, so Darwin measures the biological resultant in the form of the law of the survival of the fittest. Previous to him, biology stood much on the same level as the Ptolemaic universe which is based solely upon observation. Observation indeed permits of measurements of mass but not of measurements of force. At one bound Darwin leaps to an apprehension and treatment of biology strictly after the fashion of energetics, and thereby makes good his claim to rank with Robert Mayer and his successors. Comprehension, science, can only be carried on where there is flux, where there is change. It is the glory of the Darwinian theory that it sufficiently fluidized for thought, the world of living beings, broke up the rigid conception of species, the belief in single acts of creation, as to render them accessible to a physical mode of apprehension; the which always amounts to a mechanistic mode, to a falling, even where it calls itself the mode of energetics. His theory of natural selection is, in the strictest sense of the words, a liquidation of the inventory of antiquated ideas. But be it well noted: like the greatness of every mechanistic view, the greatness of the Darwinian thought resides in its purely re-active quality, in the fact that it only furnishes biological relation-values.

I incline to look upon the reception and interpretation which the Darwinian teaching has received at the hands of science as one of the hugest jokes world-history—taken in the biological, not the historical sense—has ever indulged in at the expense of the human mind. It is more than a joke; it is a stroke of wit! In all seriousness men wrangle as to whether Darwin's doctrine is true or false; which is the same as if they disputed, for example, about the truth or falsity of the decimal system. Men find that the longer the theory of natural selection is tested, the more frequently does it fail them; which is the same as if a man bent upon measuring everything regardless of distinctions with a yard-stick, should find, the longer he proceeds, an ever increasing number of things that do not admit of being measured by such a scale. In fine, men so comport themselves, that oftentimes one could almost wish to live sufficiently long to hear the helpless laughter of posterity. And, with it all, what erudition!

It is unfailingly interesting and instructive to observe the difference between biology and physics. In the latter is found a sort of well-bred *savoir vivre*, a clear perception of the relativity of all knowledge-values—Pontius Pilate's query translated with all the refinements of mechanistics into physicist phraseology. In the former, in modern monism, is heard the droning, "A mighty stronghold is our God," sung in unison by shepherd and sheep; wherein, to be sure, by the word "God" one does not mean that jealous God who visits the sins of the fathers upon the children, but that abstract creature of air, "the law of evolution" which in retrospective wise, seeks to avenge the follies of the children upon the fathers.

Yet once more be it said, The doctrine of the evolution of life out of one primordial form to forms that mount by degrees ever higher and higher, is of purely symbolical significance, as indeed every law is of purely symbolical significance, inasmuch as it furnishes nothing save the possibility of grouping together in one definite connection a large, nay, a limitless number of phenomena.

Of course men point to the fact that modern biology is able to bring about actual and genuine modifications in living creatures. Nothing is further from my intention than to call in question the facts connected with breeding. Daily life sufficiently proves them, and the laboratory demonstrates them under a variety of elegant and surprising forms. But what does one breed? One breeds peculiar conditions under which some life-process or other runs its course—never by any means the process itself—in the selfsame way that the physicist "breeds" the sunbeam as a spectrum, as a polarised ray, as interference, and so forth. Never yet has breeding brought about the transmutation of one life-form into another higher in the scale of being.

Now comes the moment when the evolution theorist plays out his last and highest trump. "Very good!" he says. "Let it be that in consequence of our hitherto still defective technique we have not yet succeeded in transmuting one species into a higher, nevertheless, in the facts that have been grouped together under the name of the fundamental biogenetic law and in rudimentary formations, Nature shows us that she herself has actually come this way."

Of a surety the Buddha knew of no fundamental biogenetic law, probably also had no idea of so-called rudimentary formations; but I simply cannot imagine anything that more conclusively proves the truth of his thought than these same facts. For, to him who has learned of the Buddha, these facts do not say that which the modern biologist imputes to them; they testify to the existence of *actual* associations between living beings right down into what we call the lowest stages. They bring immediately before our eyes the competency of human Kamma to find foothold outside the human kingdom also. As a traveller bears about with him this and the other trace of the dirt of the roads along which he has journeyed, so does the embryo in the various stages of its development exhibit the traces of Samsāra, demonstrate its power to take hold in the heights and in the deeps, exactly according as its Kamma is attuned, and demonstrate also that it *has taken* hold in the heights and deeps, exactly according as its Kamma *was* attuned. The embryonal forms show—to use the language of physics—the tremendous amplitude of vibration of the *I*-process. They show *that we all eat out of the one dish.*

I am quite prepared to find interpretations such as these evoke nothing but merriment among orthodox men of science. But I address myself as little to the slaves of science as to the slaves outside it. I address myself to men who think with sufficient independence and possess sufficient sense of actuality to allow facts to have unbiassed weight with them.

The following is also worthy of consideration :—

The fundamental biogenetic law, as interpreted by Haeckel is a complete contradiction of the very nature of the theory of Natural Selection. Like every purely scientific mode of envisaging things, the latter comes in on an unaccented beat, so to speak. It starts out with a given difference of potentiality, with respect to which one does nothing but observe the symptoms furnished by the process of compensation ; refraining, however, from every interpretation of how these differences could ever have arisen. In the interpretation of the evolutionist, on the other hand, the facts upon which the fundamental biogenetic law is based of necessity point in the direction of a first beginning ; they converge upon the idea of the "setting in of life." Hence they constrain to a scientific form of faith, which necessitates acrimonious warfare against the church-form of the same, if one cannot agree that the primordial cell, existing all complete, and the "In the beginning God created the heaven and the earth," may be regarded simply as different attempts at the definition of one and the same occurrence. It is the feud betwixt dog and wolf. In the dusk they might pass for mates, were it not that each is busy trying to take a bite out of the other's throat. But, like all atheists from the most ancient times, modern monism, too, forgets that to challenge the *bon dieu* to single combat is, as politicians would say, to "recognize him in principle," and that at bottom this duel can be nothing but a *modus vivendi* for both parties.

Darwin's original position entirely obviates such a strait as this. It is, as all science should be, strictly a-moral. With disconcerting—or if one likes, refreshing—coolness, the biological pieces are set up on the cosmic chess-board, and a game begun. The first move of the opening is already made, and now move after move follows of simple necessity. Where, for example, Darwin speaks of the cuckoo's instinct, he makes no attempt to account for the same by itself. He rather begins, "Now let us suppose that the ancient progenitor of our European cuckoo had the habits of the American cuckoo, and that she occasionally laid an egg in another bird's nest . . ." and so on;[1] which simply means: the game is already in full swing, and so one move follows from the other.

Darwin might be called the grand master of the art of biological chess. Nothing was further from his mind—originally at least—than turning the game to earnest; from the fact that a biological game is in progress, to seek to deduce an answer to the question as to *how* such a thing could ever have come about. That would only mean spoiling the

[1] *Origin of Species*, p. 212. John Murray, London, 1884.

whole game. And as a matter of fact, by none has it been more completely spoiled for him than by his own followers. To them it is that Bunge's words are directed: "The Darwinians teach that everything is cleared up, that only the riddle of heredity yet remains to be solved. But it is precisely this riddle of heredity which makes up the riddle the Darwinians imagine they have explained. What, then, is inherited? In the case of man there is inherited the capacity to evolve a man out of a cell. For as long as one remains unable to solve this riddle—the riddle of ontogeny—one remains still less able to solve the riddle of phylogeny."[1]

Darwin himself so chose his position that at all times he could look his God in the face. The unalleviated insipidity of his position is precisely the proof of the exact scientific form in which he—the first to do so—laid hold of the biological problem. But in this mode of laying hold of it, the fundamental biogenetic law with its various perspectives has no place whatever.

But neither do the rudimentary formations admit of being read by the Darwinian formula. They must have arisen through persistent disuse. In the mechanistic world-view, however, an arising through disuse is a sheer contradiction. Every disuse implies the presence of an arbitrary impulsion. In the strictly mechanistic apprehension of things, the whole universe in each of its impulsions is to be apprehended as the relapse of some other impulsion, that is, as process of compensation; and every deficiency of activity in this never-resting process of compensation, practically as well as theoretically,

[1] *Physiologie*, i. p. 402.

would be a miracle. As in the mechanical cosmogony of the physicist, so also in the Darwinian cosmogony, the single active impulsion in the whole mechanism remains the diversity given with the various forms of life; and as above the physical, so also here the biological event becomes simply the compensation of these countless single diversities. Hence every theory of disuse is synonymous with the introduction of a foreign, non-mechanical impulsion.

The Darwinian formula lays hold of the phenomena of life only in a certain medial tract. Somewhat as a scale of temperature-measurement lays hold of the phenomena of heat only in a certain medial tract, and above and below that tract is of no service, so the theory of natural selection is of no service as regards the fundamental biogenetic law on the one hand, and the rudimentary formations on the other.

The third and weightiest consideration, however, is this, that the fact of the formation of hybrids lies neither above nor below the scale, but altogether outside of it; following our metaphor, to apply the Darwinian idea to them would mean to seek somehow to apply the heat-scale to electric or magnetic phenomena. So soon as the evolution theory attempts to bring the fact of the formation of hybrids within its sphere of operation, it annihilates the possibility of its own existence. Natural selection is only possible in self-copulation. A self-copulation to the point of sterility is a contradiction in itself; hence Darwin himself is here obliged to have recourse to unknown impulsions. "The general sterility of crossed species may safely be looked at, not as a special acquirement or endowment, but as incidental on changes of an unknown nature in their sexual elements."[1] Again, "The extinction of species has been involved in the most gratuitous mystery. . . . We need not wonder at extinction; if we must marvel, let it be at our own presumption in imagining for a moment that we understand the many complex contingencies on which the existence of each species depends."[2] This, however, means nothing but putting the question, "Who says we have a right to inquire into everything?" And that, again, means nothing but to be a good Christian.

That, of course, is not the slightest disparagement to the teaching, so long as one takes it for what it really is—a standard of measurement for the facts, a formula by means of which one may more easily express them. It would be passing sentence of death upon it, as also upon the law of the conservation of energy, if, apprehending it in childish wise, one interpreted it as a genuine world-conception, as a law that should not merely supply a *reading* of the facts, but account for these facts themselves.

When modern biology inclines to set aside the Darwinian teaching in favour of the more novel theories of mutation, it is acting like that countryman who bought himself a pair of spectacles, expecting them not only to make print clear to his eyes but also teach him how to read, and who then made complaint that the glasses did not do their duty. The theory of natural selection, as well as every other theory, may be likened to reading-glasses. It reveals the facts in such a way as to

[1] *Origin o Species*, p. 259. John Murray, London, 1884.
[2] *Ibid.* p. 297.

lighten the labour for weakly eyes, but it does not teach one to understand the facts themselves. And as with glasses, so with theories; one has to change them, on an average, every five years.

But let us return to our subject proper.

Here also the Buddha supplies a single concept in the place of two miracles. That to which science gives the name of rudimentary organs are here not the results of continuous disuse—once more I ask, how in a purely mechanical apprehension of things disuse can ever set in at all—but, precisely the same as the facts of the fundamental biogenetic law, they are witnesses to a beginningless journey up and down throughout the entire domain of living creatures. In the place of the double miracle—a threatened absolute beginning in the facts of the fundamental biogenetic law, and a threatened absolute end in the fact of rudimentary organs—one single concept! And the formation of hybrids is here robbed of all its danger. Beings are neither heirs of their progenitors nor bequeathers to their posterity; they are heirs of themselves.

In such a mode of apprehending life, that which we basely and vulgarly call co-ition acquires a meaning of its own. Again there is that delicate irony that comes only of commanding height of position. The intercourse of the sexes is only the *attempt* at co-ition, at coming together. In plain truth, both man and woman are nothing but the surrogates of nature, which makes use of them in order to render possible the real co-ition, the conflux of Kamma and its material. Hence, species and sub-species count for nothing. Such a "something" as species is nowhere to be found in actuality. It is nothing but a way of apprehending the phenomena of life.

It may be rejoined, "But as a matter of fact beings are so constituted as to admit of their being grouped together into species. This is so in the scientific apprehension of things, where the new being is exclusively derived from the material of the parents, in accordance with nature. But in the Buddhistic apprehension of things, there is no reason whatever why two living beings, so far as form is concerned, should be like one another at all."

To this, reply may be made, Two living beings exactly alike as to form are not to be found. Groupings, of no matter what kind, are always matters of accommodation; which means that they are only made possible by the neglecting of trifling divergencies. The fool in *King Lear*, informing us why the Pleiades has seven stars, says, "Because there are not eight of them." There are not eight of them, however, not because an eighth is not there, but just because we leave out the remainder, do not count them in. So also is it with species. Of course, I am never in any doubt as to what it is that I name man, dog, cow, and so forth, for these concepts have first been settled by myself. But as that which I comprehend with my horizon changes content at every step I take, so also do the concepts man, dog, and so forth. Everything is comprehended in an uninterrupted self-accommodation, self-attunement, each after other, that only runs its course with sufficient sluggishness, provisionally to render possible and justify the groupings of natural science in order to better understanding. To ask why precisely there are the forms that there are, is to ask why in general there is anything given at all. It simply is so! The question would have some meaning were stationary forms here present from eternity and to eternity. But all these forms are nothing but a perpetual forming itself into itself from beginninglessness down to the present moment. To say that there is a world, a reality at all, is to say that there *must* be resemblances. Otherwise a self-attunement of energy and material were utterly impossible. The resemblances, and therewith in the second place the possibility of classific syntheses are real and conceptual *preliminary condition* of all actuality—yea, actuality itself.

Another objection which every thinking man must make is one that out of prudence is raised by the theory of descent itself. It is this: "How can the theory of a gradual unbroken ascent in the evolutional series be reconciled with the simultaneous existence of the lowest alongside of the highest forms?" Here the theory of descent is unable even to make an attempt at a satisfactory explanation. Darwin himself on this point says, "Such objections as the above would be fatal to my view, if it included advance in organization as a necessary contingent."[1] This declaration throws a flood of clearest light upon Darwin's whole attitude towards the theory of evolution, and at the same time upon the arbitrariness with which he has been interpreted by his followers.

Now let us consider the other side. The Buddha-thought, regarded from the physiological

[1] *Origin of Species*, p. 308.

position, is based upon the insight that every living being is a singly determined existence. The question is, Are there facts in nature which would contradict this one and single determination?

I confine myself to the most promising instance, that of the amœba multiplying themselves by fission. This fact, interpreted according to science, would mean that here energy divides itself, exists alongside itself, since Weissman says that at the moment of partition neither of the two cells, if "endowed with self-consciousness," could say which was mother and which daughter. "I have no doubt that each half would look upon the other as the daughter, and itself as the original individual," he says in his *Dauer des Lebens*.

Were there any real necessity to compel such an interpretation, then the single determination of energies would be riddled through and through. But there is no compelling necessity, nay, nor even possibility, of interpreting what happens after such a fashion. One is equally entitled to say that in the sundered sections a new energy lays hold. That this daughter-section continues its movements without a break is no proof of the orthodox conception of what takes place. The human sperm-cell, after its expulsion from the old organism, also for a longer time retains its own particular movements. It works itself towards the ovum against the vibratory movements of the epithelium; thus, so to speak, against the stream.

Incidentally it may be remarked that this fact alone, interpreted according to physiology, would give rise to a difficulty that must render insoluble the entire problem of fecundation. For this movement of the sperm-cell renders necessary the question, "When precisely does the actual moment of fecundation occur? Is it at the first signs of conception? or at the moment when the sperm-cell penetrates the sheath of the ovum? or at the moment of their first mutual contact? or has not fecundation already virtually set in with this endeavour of the sperm-cell to get to the ovum-cell?" One might then inquire, after the fashion of jurists: "At what moment precisely is the deed born? Is it when I carry it out? or when I get ready to carry it out? or when I form the resolve to carry it out?" Such are the difficulties that arise when one seizes the problem of procreation in a purely materialistic way. And one is bound to seize it in a purely materialistic way if one would seize it scientifically.

A single fact which contradicts the unique determination of a living being is not to be found, and never can be found. For this, it would be necessary that energy itself should be accessible, seizable by sense; and that is a contradiction in itself. One energy only is accessible—my consciousness. And this is *the* uniquely determined.

So much for the attitude of the Buddha-thought to the biological problem. To procure acceptance for such views, a broad high-way would first need to be driven through the jungle of scientific opinions. Science divides consciousness and life, making the former merely an accident of the latter, and seeking and seeing it only in the line of matter. The processes of fission in unicellular organisms call up visions of an "eternal life." Thereupon men halt and say with full conviction—and justification also,

"The continuity of consciousness is apparently interrupted; the continuity of life is never interrupted";[1] or else, "It is no cell-complex that dies, but a concept";[2] in saying which, so far as the form of the words goes, they entirely agree with the Buddha, and yet in meaning stand so desperately far from him that every hope of an understanding between them is out of the question.

This inward divergence reveals itself here and there in the *sequelæ*: All the facts connected with the doctrine of generation and the history of evolution, which in the scientific mode of envisaging them become insoluble problems, with the Buddha are all resolved in *one* thought—that of individual beginninglessness represented by the line of Kamma, and so become *the evangel of a new world-conception.*

[1] Bunge's *Physiologie.*

[2] Weissman's *Leben und Tod.*

X

BUDDHISM AND THE COSMOLOGICAL PROBLEM

THIS problem treats of the question as to the arising of the world in general and life in particular—thus, has its foundation in the methodical play against one another of two absurdities; as indeed follows from the possibility of reversing the positions. If the materialist asks, "How has life come into the world?" the idealist equally inquires, "How has the world entered into life, *i.e.* into me, into my consciousness?" From the outset, it is obvious that here both are provided with unlimited scope for the performance of mental feats worthy to rank on equal terms with the derring-do of a "raging Roland." And as the Duke of Florence asked of the worthy Ariosto, "Messer Ludovico, where ever did you learn all those tricks?" so here, in similar wise, one might ask, "Master of the lecture-room, master of the crucible and the retort, where ever did you learn all those tricks?"

For biologist and physicist the train of reasoning here runs as follows:—

"Life is present! Proof: I, the thinker!" The first rule of play in the cosmic game, according to scientific principles, is: "God" does not count—just as in a vaulting contest the stick does not count. This granted, the whole problem embodies itself in these two possibilities:—

(*a*) Has life arisen through spontaneous generation? (*b*) Has it descended hither from beginninglessness?

The question of spontaneous generation has undergone manifold vicissitudes. Aristotle made use of spontaneous generation with perfect ingenuousness, not to say unstinted lavishness. The more, however, continued experiment taught that where one had hitherto imagined one beheld the arising of new life, serious mistakes had been made—that germs of life had found their way into the medium, all the more did men turn away from the idea of a *generatio spontanea*. The experiments of Pasteur seemed to give the decisive blow. Wherever life is present, life is presupposed.

To-day men give their opinion on the subject of the possibility of spontaneous generation with that cautious reserve which has been learnt from the calculation of probabilities.

A modern physiologist expresses himself as follows:—

"The question as to whether out of dead substance a living cell can be produced, whether so-called spontaneous generation is a possibility, does not in the present condition of our knowledge permit of being answered in a decided negative. We are bound to admit the possibility, even though all experiments yield a negative result."[1]

The necessity which, despite all negative results,

[1] G. v. Bunge, *Physiologie*, i. p. 361.

compels one to cling to the possibility of spontaneous generation, is the truly heroic violence with which biology identifies "life" and "cell."

The entire sum of biological wisdom comes to a point in the saying, *Omnis cellula e cellula*—against which as little objection is to be urged as against the statement of the fact that every living being arises from another living being.

At this point, however, geology steps in and plays the spoil-sport by producing indubitable proofs of the one-time molten condition of our globe, thereby setting an insurmountable limit to "life" in the biological acceptation of the word.

This fact served as spur to all sorts of attempts at imparting a more scientific character to the belief in spontaneous generation.

In these endeavours the main support received came from organic chemistry.

The first achievement on the road to the chemical "synthesis" of life was Wöhler's demonstration of artificial urea. But this event has been so far outstripped that to-day one only looks back at it in order to bring visibly before the eye the progress that has been made in a comparatively short space of time. To-day one is already beginning to talk of the possibility of producing living albumen.

The following passage from Huxley's *On our knowledge of the causes of the phenomena of organic nature* may serve as a sample of the "scientific circumspection" with which one sets to work upon this most difficult of tasks also.

After laying it down that there are two possible proofs of the origin of life: first, the historical one as found in geology; and second, that derived from experiment—of which the former is unsatisfactory and the latter not carried out, the writer proceeds:—

"To enable us to say that we know anything about the experimental origination of organization and life, the investigator ought to be able to take inorganic matters, such as carbonic acid, ammonia, water, and salines, in any sort of inorganic combination, and be able to build them up into protein matter, and then that protein matter ought to begin to live in an organic form. That nobody has done as yet, and I suspect it will be a long while before anybody does do it. But the thing is by no means so impossible as it looks; for the researches of modern chemistry have shown us—I won't say the road towards it, but, if I may so say, they have shown the finger-post pointing to the road that may lead to it."

O agnus dei! lend me but a little of thy lamb's patience, that so I may be able to smile at this tangle of profound absurdities, this *docta ignorantia*. And this they call weighing a difficult problem with "scientific circumspection"! It is not difficult, God wot, to be circumspect when it is the purely imaginary that is in question. For the famous Monsieur "Life" of whose organization and structure mention is made above has precisely as much actuality as that Mr. Table d'Hôte for whom the farmer from the country inquired. Such a being is the most effective of subjects for science, for it admits of being solved without remainder in learnedness. *Quousque tandem professores!*

No physicist would be so irrational as to say, "I see the wind—in the swaying bough of a tree and so forth; I hear, smell, feel, measure it; but where now is he—this Mr. Wind himself?" The biologist, however, manages to say, "I see, hear, smell, taste, touch, think life; but where now is that unknown god 'Life' himself?" Once for all, Man, know that thy seeing, hearing, smelling, tasting, touching, thinking—even were they biological tricks such as thine—are life itself; other life there is not. To seek to have it issue like some homunculus from the retort or the incubator—this oughtest thou rather to leave to the other poets—the genuine ones!

It is far from my intention to embark upon polemics; but it is well-nigh impossible to pass anywhere near folly when it masquerades in the black of the most profound seriousness and resist the temptation to give it a good push, so that the public, by the fluttering of the rags, may recognize the hollow scarecrow. But after all, there is some sense in everything, even if this "sense" is oftentimes "non-sense!"

This is one of the attempts made to bring life—as "cell"—and the facts of geology into harmony. The other runs as follows:—

Force and matter are imperishable: it is only the form that changes. The world of astronomy displays this beginninglessness in the form of the ceaseless mutation of the heavenly bodies. Accordingly, organic life also must be beginningless, not as a sort of mystic primeval slime but as a something formed, as a cell or group of cells. Consequently it is only a question of explaining how life could find its way over from a worn-out world into a youthful one just solidifying from the molten state.

This theory presents a good example of how similarity of sound may conceal complete difference in sense.

Like the Buddha, this theory, too, teaches the beginninglessness of organized life. But whilst with the Buddha there is an actual new arising as flames arise new, by an energy encountering the material, "striking in," here there is only an inept pushing back of the facts perceptible to sense; in which latter procedure meteorites are made to serve as a sort of cosmic jam-jar, the precious stuff "life," in a conserved condition, so to speak, being passed over therein from one world to another.

A variation of this problem is the question as to whether "life" has arisen on the earth in one single place, or in several places simultaneously.

In the Buddha-thought all such questions are reduced to impotence.

The Buddha teaches:—

There are countless worlds; and as here on our world things may be destroyed by fire or water, or otherwise, so also with the worlds in space.

But as the disintegration of anything here on the Earth only means its reintegration anew in some other place, so also is it with the worlds. Nothing is destroyed, nothing perishes: it is only that a change takes place in the centres of tension—nothing more. An Earth, a Sun, a Jupiter, a Sirius, and so forth, as identities, as corporealities complete in themselves—these as little exist as there exist identities as personalities. Even as here, so also in the infinitudes of space, there are condensations having their foundation in definite energical tensions which, for the sake of easier comprehension and because the process runs its course at a rate of speed sufficiently low, we designate by the names of Earth, Sun, Jupiter Sirius, and so forth. Like every *I*-process that presents itself to my senses, they possess significance only as symptoms; they are nothing but forms in which certain definite energies make themselves manifest.

In the Buddha's system there are no such things as worlds in themselves. A world is nothing but the summation of the single processes of which it is made up, just as a banquet is nothing but the summation of the guests and the ingredients of the feast. As birds flock together because there is something present that attracts them in large numbers; as crows gather round a mango-stone; as a saline solution from the centre of shock outwards proceeds to crystallize; so does this unitary experience, whether it manifest itself in organic or non-organic shape, conglobate into cosmic groups, burst into systems of worlds. Here one must hold to it firm and fast that "non-organic" is not the converse of "organic," but is simply the not organic, and an indication that energies are here concerned upon which we ourselves even by analogy can say nothing.[1] For the rest, however, all is the same—all is the self-interweaving of energy and material—all is Saṅkhāra. Whether the processes are of such a nature as in the course of their development to permit of flowering forth into consciousness or whether they are not—this makes no essential difference. When the Buddha says: "The arising of the world will I teach you," and then proceeds with his sequence of thought: "Where the eye

[1] Cf. Essay IX.

and forms are, there arises visual consciousness; the conjunction of the three results is contact; contact yields feeling," and so on; or when he says: "The world is where the six senses are"—this is not meant in the philosophical idealistic sense. There is no arising of the world other than that experienced at every moment as a self-interweaving of energy and material in me, in every being, in every process in the world. *The summation of this individual experience—that is the world.* Other world there is not. This moment that now says "*I*"—this is the arising of the world, and never and nowhere in all the universe does it take place otherwise. As eater, as self-nourisher, I am *world-maker* in the strictest sense of the word. In this actual world nothing new arises. Centres of tension, tendencies, shift about hither and thither, heave up and down like mist-wreaths over the dark depths of unfathomable abysses—a beginningless coming together, a beginningless falling asunder, in which nothing persists save the never-sated thirst, the ever-sleepless lust for food. It is the terrible game "law" that here is played. Worlds, the arena; fates, the players; and the prize—nothing!

In connection with such a beginningless integration and disintegration, to speak of a condition of greater or lesser development is the notion of a child. As little as the clenched fist is more developed than the five fingers outspread, just as little is a world in space peopled with thinking, living beings more developed than one spread out in masses of nebula; all things are only phases in a beginningless proceeding here presenting itself to me symptomatically, but of which I obtain a direct comprehension in consciousness. To ask whether suns and Milky Ways are without beginning is meaningless; for they are positively nothing else but the expression of the hither and thither movement of energies; but that which I now experience in consciousness, that is—rightly considered—beginninglessness itself; and the self-integration and self-disintegration of worlds is nothing but the functional concomitant phenomenon of the beginninglessness of the *I*.

If now such a Lokadhātu (world-system) goes to decay, this, conformable to its nature, is nothing but a summation of single dyings. The Kamma of the single things takes fresh hold in the universe there where it can take hold—and therefore *must* take hold. Actual energies take hold immediately, independent of space and time. There is no need to trace their course from meteorites and cosmic nebulæ, from one heavenly body to another, somewhat as one might trace a letter from its place of postage to its destination; but even as our thoughts are immediate, independent of time and space, as our loves are able to "lay hold" in the remotest ends of the earth, so do the Kammas lay hold immediately, independent of time and space, in the most distant abysses of infinitude, even to where no light-year any more can measure—lay hold there, whither, in virtue of their propensities, their tendencies, they reach out.

From the commanding position of such a conception it follows that Buddhist cosmogony does not fit in with our crude astronomical ideas. As it is not always the case that "birds of a feather flock together"—there are solitary denizens of air, noble creatures that wing their way through the ether alone—so Buddhist cosmogony makes mention of solitary beings who segregate themselves at the initial beginnings of a new world.

When, after the break-up of a system of worlds, here and there worlds again begin to form, to sprout; when again here and there energies take hold even because they can take hold, then these beings appear as pure creatures of light, self-luminous, wheeling through boundless space, through boundless epochs of time, compact all of light, compact all of bliss, yet even as we, belonging to the world, differing only in the circumstances and antecedent conditions of their "taking hold."

One reads of this in the colossal thought-symphony of the Brahmajāla Sutta of the *Dīgha Nikāya*. It is thus that a spirit speaks who has burst through the barriers of self-imposed conceptions and unimpeded launches out into the infinitudes where thought finds never a bound save that itself enjoins, nor any halt save that it sets itself.

In conclusion I recapitulate:—

Like all the other problems of science, this too is of a dialectical nature. One is operating with one identity "world" and another identity "life," and afterwards strives in vain to bring the two into comprehensible association. In the simple entertaining of such ideas one has cut oneself off from every possibility of a solution. There is no identity "world," no identity "life." There are nothing but self-sustaining, *i.e.* beginningless processes which here and there group themselves into systems of worlds. If one has comprehended the whole world as Saṅkhāra, there is no cosmological problem. World and life are there as the beginningless unity of "processioning."

As a working hypothesis, what service is here rendered by the Buddha-thought?

The Buddha-thought explains how it comes to seem as if life had a first beginning upon a world. For as a matter of fact there is such a first beginning, and it permits of being proven historically and geologically. All this is beyond possibility of dispute: it is only the interpretation that is mistaken. This first beginning is such, much in the same way that the spring welling from the rock is the first beginning of the river. It is the first beginning only where one objectifies the river as an identity. If science seeks to explain the first beginning of life by spontaneous generation, she resembles a man who should derive the spring from the rock itself. If she seeks to derive the first beginning of life from other worlds, she then is like a man who would fain derive the spring as such, as an abstract objectified something, from one or another of various localities. Only in the Buddha-thought is the first beginning of life conceived of in a genuinely cosmogonical manner, as form of the play of world-events. It is no migration of duly shaped and formed "spring"-elements, which out of atmospherical vapour and the waters of the sea fashion a spring, but a self-displacement of centres of energy. In the self-same way it is no migration of life-elements hither out of other worlds, but a self-displacement of centres of energy, which makes it that life "sprouts" anew upon a world. Here, to speak about a first beginning as such, and consequently of a condition of greater or lesser development, has about as much meaning as if one should speak of a condition of greater or lesser development in the case of the waters of the ocean, the vapour of the atmosphere, the fountain on the hill. What is true with reference to science's problem of heredity is even more true of her cosmological problem: it is wholly Hebraic.

XI

BUDDHISM AND THE PROBLEM OF THOUGHT

THE fact that a world exists simultaneously involves its existence *as such*, *i.e.* as our idea.

All speculations and theories about the world are thus of a secondary nature. Their existence were a sheer impossibility if the world, apart from its being in existence at all, were not also existent *as such*, as idea, conceptually.

In the foreword to his *Kritik der reinen Erfahrung*, R. Avenarius says:—

"This work makes the attempt to comprehend all theoretical relations whatsoever . . . as consequences of one single, simple postulate."

This "single, simple postulate for all theoretical relations" is the *possibility* of such a thing, *i.e.* the fact that conscious ideas, concepts, exist. *The concept is the problem of all thought*; and to seek to master the world epistemologically before one has mastered the concept, is sheer waste of time.

Now, in the matter of concept thought is in this awkward plight, that the former offers nothing objective that can be made to serve as a point of departure in any possible attempt at comprehension.

This simple consideration alone implies that every attempt to come at the fact "concept" inductively, *i.e.* with the implements of science, is hopeless, indeed absurd. And each fresh attempt in that direction only supplies another proof of the truth of the Buddha's teaching that all mental life perforce is bound up with ignorance as to itself.

In what follows I shall endeavour very briefly to sketch the various mistaken paths that here have been traversed.

As everywhere, so also with regard to the fact "concept," the two antitheses faith and science stand ranged over against each other. As everywhere, so also here, the fact "concept" presents no problem to faith. Just because I am endowed with a soul, a "force in itself," I possess the power, the ability to form concepts. As everywhere, so also here, the paradoxical character of faith makes itself palpably manifest: the fact of the formation of concepts is by it accepted as proof that an inconceivable in itself must be present.

Opposed to it stands science, which seeks to explain and is bound to explain how such an occurrence as the formation of concepts has ever been able to come about. Her task falls into two main divisions. On the one hand, there is the demonstrating of the subjective, antecedent conditions of the concept; this is done in the physiology of the different organs of sense. On the other hand, there is the demonstrating of the objective, antecedent conditions of the concept—objects, the external world.

Of this task the subjective part, and the entire fruitlessness of the same, have already been dealt with in another place. The objective division comprehends philosophy in the broadest sense of the word. For every theory and speculation as to the world may without exception be traced back to this one question: "How must the world be fashioned to render possible the fact that consciousness-contents, conscious ideals, concepts, exist—in fine, that the world exists *as such*?" In this question is comprehended all philosophy, as the tree is comprehended in the root.

All the theories as to the constitution of the world that have ever been advanced or that will ever be advanced, branch into these two fundamental views:—

First: the view that at the foundation of things there exists a constant in itself, an unconditioned constant, an identical with itself, or whatever else one has a mind to name it.

Second: the view that there exists no such unconditioned constant at the foundation of things, but that all that exists is merely a relation-value, and that the one single constant in the universe is the constant of relations formulated abstractly in scientific law.

Now, to the impartial observer the world presents itself in a twofold aspect: on one hand as "something that is," and on the other as "something that happens." In the former of these two fundamental views, things would be something that *has* happening, something that has this happening proceed forth from it. In the latter view, things would *be* the happening itself, would resolve themselves completely into happening.

As already set forth at length in what has gone

before, this latter conception is that given for science as the mechanical world-theory. Science, if she would justify her title to the name, dare not accord recognition to anything concealed behind things, anything imperceptible to sense. If this be granted, "that which is" then becomes purely a form of "that which happens," and the universe in its entirety one huge mass of relation-values. For a thing is perceptible to sense and therewith apprehensible only in so far as it enters into relations with other things, which includes, with my senses.

Any third view is impossible, for, from the strictly epistemological standpoint, opposites, between them, always comprehend the whole. From the standpoint of strict epistemology, with any kind of thing as a concept—with the concept "tree" for example—all the rest of the world is given as "not-tree"—so completely given with it that the interpolation of any third concept is an utter impossibility.

It may be asked, "In what do these two opposed fundamental views find their justification?"

All things exist for us only in so far as they are perceptible to us. They exist as appearances, as the sum of their properties. If now the thinking mind would have anything made wholly manifest, wholly perceptible to sense—would seek to have something made wholly and entirely *appearance*, there always remains a residue that refuses to be made manifest, refuses to be made perceptible to sense. Speaking generally, one may say: Applied thought seems to conduct to a something lying at the foundation of things, to a constant in itself, of which all properties, all in things that is perceptible to sense, are only so many different expressions. The idea that all that exists does so in virtue of a constant in itself, presents itself as a *necessity of thought*, which science must oppose by every means if she would retain her title to the name of science.

Since this constant in itself is of necessity an imperceptible to sense, it imposes no restrictions upon apprehension. One is perfectly at liberty to conceive of it in quite contrary forms—as matter or substance, equally as well as under the form of force. If one holds by the former mode of conceiving it, then, whatever the guise its elaboration in thought may assume, one belongs to the school *of materialism*. If, on the contrary, one holds by the latter mode of apprehension, one then belongs, quite independent of the form its detailed elaboration in thought may assume, to the *idealistic* school. For the correct appraisement of our whole mental life, however, it is important clearly to understand that the opposition is only an apparent one. Both alike have one common root in the idea of an *unconditioned constant* lying at the foundation of things, which, summed up, may be designated as *the substans* (*das Substans*) of all appearances. *The substance*, accordingly, results purely as the material form of this *substans*, while the force represents its immaterial form : the one being as well—and as ill—authenticated as the other, since one knows nothing of either, nor ever can know anything.

If now one follows up the various transformations that have taken place in this domain within historical times, one finds that, as is also the case in the domain of natural science, they occur following the law of the *inversion of positions.* Does the one school, whether it be the materialistic or the idealistic, force its way into such a preponderating position as to become intolerable to sound common-sense, it is forced to give place to its opponent, which then for a season takes the lead, only, after a longer or shorter period, to undergo a like fate. It is like a game of see-saw. All the acuteness, all the profundity, all the mental florescence which the one school has manifested in the course of centuries of labour perhaps, in this period of decline are brought to destruction, and only by ardent collectors can be rescued and preserved as a palæontological form of mental life. At bottom, the whole of philosophy up to each new "now" is nothing but a more or less tastefully-arranged palæontological collection of thought-values.

Above and alongside this play of inversions betwixt idealism and materialism—which I might call the inversion of the *lower order*—there takes place another inversion of a *higher order.*

In certain intervals the human understanding begins to offer serious resistance to both the world-views that base themselves on the concept of *substans* in its two possible forms—that of substance and that of force—by hastening over to one that is the contrary of both, a world-conception from which *substans* is wholly absent, a world consisting entirely of a mass of relation-values. This latter form of world-conception alone has the right to the designation of "scientific." For there can be no science, properly so-called, where the subject dealt with is any shape or form of an imperceptible to sense.

Now, the first inversion of the higher order with which we in our Western circles of culture are acquainted has, to be sure, a slight enough scientific cast. It is the inversion that set in with Protagoras the Sophist. With his thesis, "Man is the measure of all things—of those that are, that they are; of those that are not, that they are not"—he places himself in an attitude of opposition to both world-conceptions founded on the concept of *substans*; for in both these conceptions things, as existing in virtue of an unconditioned constant, must also be the measure of man.

The appearance of Protagoras was a naturally-resulting protest against the absurdities to which materialism and idealism had mutually driven each other. The former found its culminating point in Democritus of Abdera, who left nothing in the world but matter in the shape of atoms. The latter reached its corresponding culmination in Plato, who left nothing in the world but the immaterial *substans*, ideas, to whom thereby matter became the non-existent.

The whole procedure of Protagoras conveys the impression that his inversion was of a purely dialectical nature. For the style and manner in which he formulates his new point of view leaves to humanity for all its mental life nothing but mere opinion. His dictum as to man being the measure of all things takes no account of a natural order of things. To this perhaps may be attributed the fact that his philosophy, however arresting it may have been in his own day and time, set forth personally by this gifted mind, has yet proved itself to be but little permanent.

After the see-saw between idealism and materialism had proceeded for some two thousand years more, the new inversion of the higher order set in with a mighty whirlwind, the most powerful, the most systematically-delivered attack upon the notion of *substans* that Western philosophy had ever experienced—the philosophy of Hume.

Hume's philosophy, briefly stated, consists in the investigation of what exhibits itself to sense-perception considered as based on a possible content of *substans*—in unravelling it to the last thread and pointing out to his contemporaries with irrefutable clearness and acuteness, "See there, you people! a constant in itself is nowhere to be found!"

Hume is frequently alluded to as a sceptic. I consider, on the contrary, that his philosophy is the purest criticism precisely where in philosophy criticism may be practised at all—namely, upon the concept of *substans*, whether in material or immaterial form.

Every criticism of *substans* culminates naturally in criticism of the notion of an *I*. For Hume, the *I*, the self, became a bundle, a collection of separate mental representations "that follow one another with inconceivable rapidity and are in a state of perpetual flow, continual motion."

But a criticism of the notion of *substans* is incomplete without a criticism of the concept of cause; for the intuition that all that exists must have an adequate cause is likewise a necessity of thought. Now, where there is a constant in itself, a *substans* in things, causality is an actual *following after one another* of cause and effect, this "constant in itself" being also "cause in itself" of that which happens, the latter therefore, as "effect in itself," representing a simple following upon that cause in itself, in such sort that between the two there exists a necessary—I might almost say—a rigid dependence; whereupon the question, "How is a relation between the two possible?" becomes a problem that defies solution.

Hence it follows that one is bound to hold the problem of causality as a correlate of *substans*. If the latter falls, the former falls along with it.

As the notion of a constant in itself becomes in the criticism of Hume a simple product of imagination, so for him does the concept of causality become the simple outcome of use and wont. Because in our representation of things we frequently observe two things to follow one upon the other, we assume that a necessary dependence exists between the two. Hume solves both these problems by declaring them, without a moment's hesitation, to have no existence at all.

After Hume, the see-saw game of the lower order went on for a time. Upon the intellectual materialism of the eighteenth century—especially as it prevailed in France, where it was represented by such men as La Mettrie and Von Holbach—there followed the idealism of Fichte, Schelling, and Hegel. After this had exploded of its own gaseousness, the scientific materialism of the nineteenth century set in, and up to our day has continued to hold the upper hand, though now it seems to be swinging back in a new idealistic movement.

Alongside of this a new inversion of the higher order has managed to prepare itself, making its appearance in two distinct forms, of which one is the direct successor of the criticism of Hume, while the other derives from physics.

The former is modern positivism, as developed in particular by Ernst Mach and R. Avenarius. The latter is the so-called world-theory of energetics, as represented more especially by Ostwald the physicist.

Both schools partake of a purely scientific character in so far as they aim at furnishing world-theories from which a *substans* is ruled out—seek to frame a world consisting solely of relation-values, a world in which the one thing constant is the constancy of the relations.

A third school, modern monism, as represented especially by Haeckel, is not scientific at all.

As already said, it is of the essence of every scientific view that it should apprehend the entire play of world-events purely as relation-values. Such a world-conception is bound always to set out from the midst of the play of events, with things already in full swing. Modern monism, with its teaching of primordial life in the form of a primordial cell or some other primordial form, is science only in outward appearance; at the core it is unmitigated superstition, and ought to be regarded as such by every thinking man, for it betrays itself such by its uncritical abuse of ecclesiastical dogma.

After this historical review, given with the utmost possible brevity, we have to inquire:—

What is the reason then for this insufficiency of the *substans*-views, whether it refer to a material or to an ideal *substans* in things? Why are materialism and idealism alike devoid of any kind of demonstrative ability?

The answer to this is :—

Because both alike are hampered by a contradiction within themselves. This contradiction becomes manifest in the fact that such a world as would be yielded by the concept of *substans* would be so constituted that in it the fact "concept," *i.e.* the fact that a world exists as idea, would be bound to remain an eternally insoluble problem.

This necessarily results from the following considerations :—

If there is any *substans* lying at the foundation of things, it must be a "constant in itself"; as such, however, it must be something possessing no possibility whatever of entering into relations with other things, in any kind of way. If it cannot do this, neither can it become perceptible to sense. If it does not become perceptible to sense, it cannot become a content of consciousness.

Here it may be said: "But it is not *substans* itself, but its expressions, *i.e.* things, in so far as they are properties, functions, that enter into relations, whether with other things or with the organs of sense of living beings." But from this we could never get anything else but a summation of disconnected sense-impressions. The thread, so to speak, needed to string the sense-impressions together into a complete, coherent, mental representation would be missing. Everything, so far as it exists for me as a concept, would have to be the expression precisely of a *substans* lying at its foundation. But to possess a conscious mental representation of this as an unconditioned constant is a contradiction in itself. Hence the fact that there are concepts, *i.e.* that a world as such exists, *i.e.* that there is a world at all, is a direct contradiction of the idea of a *substans* in virtue of which things are supposed to have existence. With the admission of this idea, every possibility of understanding how such a thing as a content of consciousness ever could come to be, is wholly excluded.

In point of fact, all life, within the boundaries of materialism and idealism, exhausts itself in fruitless attempts to furnish more or less ingenious explanations to account for the connection between the physical and the psychical. Hence the perpetual game of see-saw between both, and the utter inadequacy of either to the genuine thinker, however much ability may be displayed within the limits of the position chosen. All becomes valueless, because the outcome of a presupposition that is a standing contradiction of itself.

And now, how stands it here with the view of the world from which *substans* is absent?

As already said: Where the idea of *substans* is torn out of the play of world-events, nothing remains but a world of pure relation-values wherein the one thing constant is the constancy of the relations.

Now, every relation is precisely the inconstant, the unstable, in itself. The heat that springs up with the friction of two objects may—nay, *must* be looked upon as a relation-value springing up anew with each new moment. Every moment may be represented as consisting of an infinite number of fractions of a moment; in short, it is the unstable in itself.

If now one apprehends the whole play of world-events as relation-values, thereby not only do the phenomena resulting from the play of things upon one another, but also the things themselves, become simple relation-values, and so also examples of the unstable in itself.

Into anything by nature an unstable, connection can only enter through me, the beholder, introducing it in my comprehension of the same. Here the binding thread is lacking in things themselves; with the idea "pure relation-values" one has pulled it out oneself, as is proven by modern positivism itself, even if unwittingly, when it seeks to replace the old succession of cause and effect by the timeless function-concept of mathematics—a thing possible only where the actual cohesion is absent.[1]

With this, however, one stands in a position of contradiction to oneself, *i.e.* to actuality. For if the whole play of world-events, without any exception, is only a relation-value, then I myself am a relation-value also. But if that were so, "memory" would be impossible. In "memory" I *experience* the cohesion of myself, and through myself prove to myself that I am not a mere relation-value. As such—as Hering rightly remarks in his lecture *Das Gedächtnis*—our consciousness would consist of just as many splinters as one could count moments; which is simply an analytical mode of expression for the fact that there would be no consciousness at all. This in turn would mean that there could be no world *as such*, as our mental representation. And this in its turn would mean that there could be no world at all. For it is absurd to speak of a world where there is no consciousness in which it is represented as such. Without consciousness, how-

[1] Cf. Essay V., remarks on the causal sequence.

ever it might run its course, experience would know nothing of itself.

The conception of a world-theory devoid of *substans* thus also terminates in a contradiction in itself, even as those world-theories which operate with the conception of a *substans*.

As a matter of fact, every scientific view of the world demonstrates its inadequacy in respect of this first question in that it answers it in a manner against all common-sense without itself observing that this is so.

According to the view of science, concepts have their origin in experience and come to be through the discarding, the letting drop, of the unessential. But in order that a concept may come into existence after such a fashion, it is necessary that it exist beforehand as a thing given, in the same way that a statue can only come forth from out the block of marble through the discarding of the unessential, when it is already given ideally in the mind of the artist.[1]

As already remarked, all attempts to frame a view of the world upon purely scientific lines, to comprehend the play of world-events as simple relation-values, present themselves in a twofold form. Making physics its point of departure and from thence working its way forward, one view endeavours to prove the law of the conservation of energy valid also for non-reversible processes; this is the world-theory of energetics. The other view

[1] It is to this effect that E. Mach expresses himself on the subject of the concept in various passages in his works—for example, in the *Wärmelehre* and *Erkenntnis und Irrtum*. Ostwald defines the concept "as a rule in accordance with which we take note of definite characteristics of the phenomenon" (*Naturphilosophie*).

follows the results of criticism; this is modern positivism.

The entire value of the world-theory of energetics is distinguished by the following consideration:—

Its axis, its thorough bass—so to speak—is the law of the conservation of energy; once this gives way, no energical world-theory is possible.

As, however, has been explained in another place, nowhere in actuality do conditions obtain corresponding to this law. Its existence merely as a possibility demands an artificial premiss—a com-completely closed system; but this exists only as an ideal ultimate concept (*Grenzbegriff*)—nowhere in actuality.

If it is desired to make use of the law of the conservation of energy with a view to erecting a world-theory thereupon, one must set up the entire universe hypothetically as a closed system in itself. The logical consequences that necessarily follow from this supposition are detailed at the close of Essay VI.

The purely ideal nature of the point of view occupied by science in this whole picture of the world is at once evident from the simple fact that, in order to maintain the constancy of the sum of energy in the universe, she here finds herself in the predicament of still having to "handle" as energy heat that no longer permits of being transformed into mechanical work—that is, heat that exists only as an empty concept.

At this stage I wish once more to insist that this entire world-theory does not at all operate with actual energies, but only with the *expression* of actual energies, with their *reaction* as presented in *work done.* It assumes work and energy to be synonymous; which is about the same as if one assumed shadow and light to be synonymous. As shadow attests nothing save that light is present, but attests this of necessity, so work attests nothing save that energy is present. Ostwald in his *Naturphilosophie*, after expressly assuming work and energy to be alike, proceeds thus:—

"With the exception of energy, all the other concepts whose importance comes second to that of the law of the conservation of energy, find their application only within a limited field of natural phenomena. Energy alone finds itself again, without exception, in all natural phenomena; that is to say, all natural phenomena permit of being ranged under the concept of energy." Further on he says: "All that we know of the external world we can represent in the form of propositions concerning actually-existing energies; hence the concept of energy proves itself in every way the most universal that science has yet framed. It comprehends not only the problem of substance, but also that of causality."

Taken literally, word for word, all this is quite correct, and yet as a whole is founded in a total misunderstanding of actuality. That all natural phenomena should admit of being ranged under the concept of energy, *i.e.* of *work done*, is due solely to the fact that *everywhere actual energies* are in activity; of these energies, however, we know nothing, absolutely nothing; and their universal presence is proven solely by the universal presence of work. And that work is only the reaction of actual energies is made evident by the fact that the one single *actual* energy we can get at—consciousness—is the one single value in the universe which never under any circumstances admits of being "read" as work.

When further on in the same volume it is said:—

"As regards the inverse endeavour to comprehend energies apart from matter, for long one dared not attempt such a thing, albeit it was soon perceived that as a matter of fact all we ever learn about the world consists solely of a knowledge of its energical relations. . . . We will, therefore, venture the attempt to build up a view of the world from which the concept of matter will be absent, a view composed exclusively of energical materials (*i.e.* of the fact *work*)," this has about as much meaning as if some one should say, "I will endeavour, out of shadows and their innumerable modifications alone, to furnish a complete theory of light." Here we have to do simply with the occurrence designated in another place as the "inversion of positions." From an extreme materialistic position one leaps at a bound into an equally extreme energical position—each position as purely dialectical as the other. If only one held by *actuality*, one would of oneself repudiate as a profitless mental diversion the very *attempt* to erect a world-theory upon such premisses. On such one may build up physical systems, achieve technical successes, measure, compute in advance—in fine, carry on scientific studies; but one thing one can never do—out of them build up a view of the world. For a view of the world in which consciousness excludes itself from that which is to be comprehended, has precisely as much value as a numerator without a denominator.

The law of the conservation of energy is purely a reading of the physical facts, *i.e.* of the play of world-events in so far as it manifests itself in the form of reversible processes—thus, as re-actual; and as such is also recognized by physicists of intelligence.[1]

At this point, however, the biologist enters and plays the part of the countryman at the theatre by taking the picture for the reality itself. He argues with that logical acuteness such as is only possible where no actuality stands in its way: "If the law of the conservation of energy is really a universal law, the life of the brain must be just as much subject to it as the reversible processes that are not dependent on time." Thus, Hering says in his lecture on "Memory" already alluded to: "(The facts of mind, consciousness, and so forth) cannot make the human body to be anything else but that which it is—a complex of matter subject to laws not to be turned aside by anything,—laws followed by the material of the stone, by the substance of the plant."

With this, however, the biologist is put in a difficult position. He is all unaware that the reversible processes are "subject" to the law of the conservation of energy, *i.e.* may be read by it, only because it is possible here to be satisfied with reactions, only because here one does not need to know anything about the energies themselves,

[1] For a correct appreciation of the law of the conservation of energy and the value of scientific laws and data in general, one should read among others Poincaré's two works: *The Value of Science*, and *Science and Hypothesis*.

because here there is no "*I*"-sayer who might raise objections to such a mode of apprehending things. The greatness, the exactitude of physics consist precisely in this, that she confines herself strictly to the realm of reactions. In the life of the brain, so far as directly manifested—as consciousness—there are no reactions. The fact "consciousness" in others is not accessible to me; and as for myself, here action and reaction always merge into one another, though I go to work with never so elaborate psycho-physiological precautions.

Hence the necessity of ever and again laying out fresh frontier domains, such as bio-chemistry, bio-kinetics, and so forth and so on, so as to be able to say with Lady Macbeth, "We are yet young in deeds!" Thus, patience! Let us but once get these new courses drawn up and then—how the results will come flowing in!

But the only new thing about these courses is the name! In truth, here as everywhere, we have to do with the old, original problem "life"—at once our hope and our despair. And to all these new courses, by means of which men hope to master the old problem, applies that answer of Pompey's favourite cook when his master marvelled at the host of different dishes, "All one meat: only the sauces are different." For it is even the same here, "All one thing: only the names are different."

After all our vain attempts to subject consciousness also to law, this remains as our final wisdom, that the mutual dependence between the mental and the material is a thing subject to law; that is, we assume as axiom to begin with, that which we are going to prove, whereby we produce nothing but a paraphrase of the Buddha-thought, nothing but a lifeless formula of the actuality itself—that the *I*-process is subordinate to no laws, can *have* no laws because it *is* law itself. And the worth of the Baconian maxim that truth may more easily come forth from error than from confusion, is here put to a severe test, for here are combined both error and confusion.

I now proceed to a brief account of the other school—that of modern positivism.

What makes this system so interesting for us is the originality of its point of departure. Despite the fact that for the most part it has been developed by a physicist, it starts with the idea, unheard-of previous to perhaps twenty-five years ago, that the next step in the progress of science is to be looked for not from physics and its methods, *i.e.* the non-personal, but from the personal, from the study of sense-perceptions.[1]

Since positivism, like every scientific world-theory, must apprehend the play of world-events purely as a sum of relation-values, one of its tasks is to come to an understanding with the concept of substance. As the direct successor of the criticism of Hume, its position with respect to the concept of substance remains the same as with Hume: the existence of such a concept is ascribed to the faculty of imagination. Because one can remove any single constituent part of a thing without the image thereof ceasing to represent the total whole and to be recognized again as such, it is assumed that all may be taken away and that

[1] Cf. Foreword to E. Mach's *Analyse der Sinnesempfindungen.*

something will still remain behind. "Thus arises the monstrous idea of a thing in itself, different from its appearance and unknowable. The thing, the body, the matter, and so on, is nothing else but the complex of colours, sounds, and so forth, nothing more than the so-called characteristics."[1]

And now it is a question of formulating a new view with respect to a world thus stripped of the concept of substance.

All previous attempts at world-theories have made shipwreck on the fact that it was impossible for them in any wise to comprehend the connection between the physical and the psychical. What is original about the onset of positivism is this, that it starts out with psycho-physical units as world-elements.

"Hence perceptions and conceptions, the will, the feelings—in brief, the entire inner and outer world—are made up of a limited number of homogeneous elements now in volatile, now in rigid combination. These elements are usually called sensations; since, however, this name already implies a one-sided theory, we prefer to speak simply of elements."[2] Again: "It is not the bodies that beget sensation but the complex of sensations (complex of elements) that fashion the bodies. If to the physicist, bodies appear to be that which is permanent, real, and sensations, on the contrary, their fleeting, transitory appearance, he forgets that all bodies are only mental symbols for complexes of sensation. . . . Thus the world for us does not consist of so many problematic

[1] E. Mach's *Analyse der Sinnesempfindungen*, p. 4.
[2] *Analyse der Empfindungen*, page 15.

beings, which through action and reaction with another equally problematic being, the *I*, beget the sensations alone accessible to us. Colours, sounds, spaces, times . . . for us are the ultimate elements whose given connection we have to investigate."[1]

This I call supplying a world-theory from the entire, completed play of world-events. The only question is, "From a mental starting-point such as this, how stands it with the fact of all facts—*I*?"

Well, it goes badly, very badly indeed, with the poor fellow! Like a lump of sugar in a big tub of water it melts away incontinent into the all. On this point one should read pages eight and nine of the *Analyse der Sinnesempfindungen*. To cite them here in full would take up too much space. The train of thought there developed concludes with the words: "Accordingly the *I* may be so extended as finally to cover and embrace the whole world."

It may be asked, "How out of this cosmic *I*-solution does the yet actually existing *I*-deposit come about?" The answer is, "Through accommodation." The *I*-concept is a convention adapted to a certain end, a procedure pertaining to the economy of thought.

"The gathering together of the elements being connected with pleasure and pain, into an ideal unit of the economy of thought, the *I*, is of the utmost significance to the intellect standing at the service of the pain-shunning, pleasure-seeking will."[2]

What attitude shall one adopt towards a structure of thought which is nothing but an ingenious description, a picture of the fact "life," whose wealth of ingenuity, however, is purchased at the

[1] *Analyse der Empfindungen*, p. 20. [2] *Ibid.*

cost of a downright, deadly indifference in respect of this same fact, *i.e.* in respect of actuality?

Epistemologically the world is as free as a bird. Any one who chooses may exercise his intellectual faculties upon it. The above view, moreover, is expressly put forward as a theory, a reading. But after all there is one requirement every theory must fulfil, and that is that it shall not contradict itself. And that this theory does in the most flagrant fashion.

Modern positivism may be briefly characterized as the application of the definition of the "concept" in general to the *I*-concept in particular. As the concept in general can be represented, "read" as a procedure appertaining to the economy of thought, so here in a frankly unexampled dis-actualizing of actuality, the *I*-concept is to be "read" as a procedure appertaining to the economy of thought. But here even the slightest attempt to think *in terms of actuality*, forthwith conducts into the absurd. For an *I*-unity must first be given in order that it may comprehend itself as an *I*-unity. On the other hand, were the *I*-concept purely a procedure in the economy of thought, what is there to prevent the thought-economy once in a while from demanding to read me as an *I*-duality? a thing that has so far never been entertained in the brains of thinking men, but only in the cells of lunatic asylums.

Positivism is overtaken by the same fate that overtakes every criticism, as, for example, that of Hume,—commonly and incorrectly called scepticism, —it finds no substratum for the *I*-concept. And the keener its search, the more critical its procedure, the more thorough its unravelling, the more is it strengthened in this its mental representation.

With this, pure criticism has no more that it can do. It must even content itself with this negative result. Positivism, however, seeks to round out this negative result into a world-theory and so obtain its world consisting of elements of sensation—a world in which there is no clearly outlined, definitely determined *I* at all.

From a starting-point of this peculiar kind there follows, on one hand, such a similarity of expression on the part of both, as to produce an almost uncanny effect. On the other hand, however, there is such a difference in essence as could scarcely be more pronounced. In brief: modern positivism is the faithful mirror-image of the Buddha-thought, and thereby accomplishes in the dis-actualizing of actuality what only thought can accomplish at all.

In the Saŋyutta Nikāya a monk asks the Buddha, "Who has contact? who has sensation?" To whom the Buddha replies, "The question is not admissible. I do not say, 'He has contact.' Did I say, 'He has contact,' then the question, 'Who has contact, Reverend Sir?' would be admissible. Since, however, I do not say so, then of me that do not speak thus, it is only admissible to ask, 'From what, Reverend Sir, does contact proceed?'"

In close correspondence with this, one reads in E. Mach's *Analyse der Empfindungen*, "If a knowledge of the continuity of the elements (sensations) leaves us unsatisfied and we ask, '*Who* has this continuity of the sensations? *who* experiences sensation?' we are dominated by the old habit of classifying each element (sensation) as an item in an unanalysed complex, and thereby unwittingly descend to the older, lower, more limited point of view."

But whilst with positivism this mode of expression proceeds from the notion of an *I* that can be "read" from the play of world-events as a unity pertaining purely to the economy of thought,—a coldly contemplative point of view—with the Buddha it issues from the idea of a beginningless, burning actuality that asserts its individual tendencies regardless of the external world. Man by his nature is an eater. To seek to dispose of him as a simple spectator is to play with concepts. All that is actual by its very nature is aliment.

Herewith, as regards the problem of the concept, we stand in presence of the Buddha-thought. Before I pass to it, however, I consider it incumbent upon me, with respect to the criticism of positivism, yet once more in this place to emphasise the fact that nothing is further from my desire than to engage in polemical discussion. As a physicist, Ernst Mach is in my opinion one of the most original, nay, perhaps the most original of the thinkers of our day and time. His *Mechanik* and *Wärmelehre* are genuine products of intellect, works of fermentative value, and in this regard rank high above the smooth classicism of an H. von Helmholtz. One only marvels the more that a mind of such calibre should be able to find pleasure in such like mental diversions.[1]

[1] Positivism itself calls attention to this quality of non-actuality in its system. In the Foreword to the second volume of R. Avenarius's *Kritik der reinen Erfahrung*, J. Petzold says, "Modern psychology is . . . characterized by the elimination from the psychic machinery of every spring of activity." Here it is as with Roland's mare in Chamisso's poem : Perfect—but dead !

When positivism says, "There is no substratum to the *I*-concept, consequently the *I*-concept is the product of fancy and 'actually' admits of being extended to cover the whole world," it is unaware that between and above the two extremes—the *I*-concept as the expression of an unconditioned constant, as a soul substance, and the *I*-concept as the expression of a fancy—there is a third alternative, the actuality itself, as pointed out and taught us by the Buddha, that *concepts do not exist at all but only the conceiving*, and that the *I*-process, albeit no unconditioned constant, dwells therein, is not on that account something dissolving over the whole world, *but is something conceiving itself at every moment of its existence*, even as the flame is a thing conceiving itself at every moment of its existence. By no inductive method can the limit of a flame be defined with regard to its environment, and yet there is such a limit, because the flame at every moment of its existence limits itself. Its very existence is just this self-limitation. In the very same way no inductive method can define the limits of the *I*-process: so far the positivists are right. But this fact by no means imports what positivism understands by it, that the *I*-process can now be dilated, spread out to any extent one chooses: it only intimates that the *I* conceives itself and *alone* conceives itself, and therefore cannot *be conceived* inductively. When a blow swishes down, even the most correct-thinking of positivists can tell whether it has struck him or not. He "conceives" himself at every moment.

Where the *I*-process is cognized as a pure process of alimentation, "conceiving" perforce receives a physo-psychical double meaning,—or rather, that unitary meaning which comprehends in itself both the physical and the psychical. All existence, whether manifesting itself objectively or subjectively, is here a "conceiving," and this unitary "conceiving," in which is comprehended the essence of all life, alike devours both—concept as thing conceived.

Where there is nothing save "conceiving," grasping the external world, there are neither concepts nor anything fixed and stable, anything corresponding to these concepts; and the purely dialectical nature of the whole problem of the "concept" at once stands revealed. Such a problem can only have being while one is working with the notion of a "conceived," which latter must always be also a "grasped," a defined, a complete in itself—in brief, an identity. Where there is nothing save processes of combustion, of alimentation, each moment of the play of world-events represents a new, unique, biological or *Kammic* value, which never before has been and never again will be. In such a universe there are no identities. Where there are no identities there are no things conceived. Where there are no things conceived there are no concepts; there is found nothing save a beginningless reaction to the outer world. And the problem "concept" presents itself as the negative of all other problems, so to speak, the latter in their totality being founded upon the idea of a something conceived, be it as a physical, be it as a physiological, biological, cosmological identity.

This is one of the points where the genuine thinker must make good his hold. It is like a rift in the clouds, through which the searching eye penetrates into a new world, passes out of a world of error in which we all see under the form of conceiving and conceived, of subject and object, into a world wherein all oppositions blazing, melt and dissolve in the beginningless glow of Becoming.

There are no concepts as there is no conceived. This idea one must thoroughly have thought out if one would understand the Buddha, his teaching, and his attitude towards certain questions.

All commonplace thinking, of scientist as of layman, takes its stand on concepts, *i.e.* operates with the notion of a conceived, with the notion of identities.

In formal logic this fact finds its due expression in the laws of identity and of contradictories. For both these laws existence is only possible where and for so long as there are things conceived, things confined, identities; they have simply no meaning with reference to an *actual* universe, a universe that is naught save a sum of combustion processes. This is the intellectual measuring-rod by which to test whether any one is thinking *in terms of actuality* or not: Do or do not the laws of identity and of contradictories hold good for his world?

Just as Aristotle reproached Heraclitus with violations of the law of contradictories,—for this really limited mind knew not, never even suspected that actuality in its entirety is nothing else but one huge violation of the law of contradictories,—just as the sun is a violation of an absolutely correct-running chronometer, so do western scholars repeatedly reproach the Buddha with violations of the law of contradictories; whereby they only prove but that they understand neither the Buddha nor actuality.

In Oldenburg's *Buddha* one reads :—

"The art of definition was something which the era of the Buddha did not possess; that of demonstration was only evolved as far as the first rudiments. An especially characteristic feature of this mode of thinking . . . is a decided antipathy to pursuing the consideration of things back to their ultimate principles."

Misericordia! What shall one say of the herd when the leading bull points in such paths! A teaching whose greatness resides in the fact that it shows how all definitions are only essays which owe their existence to the faulty formulation of the question, is reproached with its lack of definitions! A teaching which points out that the fact "*I*" of necessity implies life and the beginninglessness of life, is reproached that it does not involve itself in the blind alley of contraries called in the language of logic, "principles." The Buddha's one and only concern is to teach, to point out that there is nothing in the world to be defined; hence, also, no instruments for this purpose: principles. That herewith the whole of science goes by the board —what matters that to the seeker for truth! Hearken, good people! Here goes by the board a great deal more than science!

To see how the Buddha bore himself with reference to this question of principles, one ought to read the magnificent Kevaddha Sutta—Sutta XI. of the *Dīgha Nikāya*—where a monk craves information as to the behaviour of the primal elements of matter. The Buddha meets the question as the genuine thinker alone can, with the weapon of humour. For absurdities cannot be dealt with at all otherwise, if one would not drown in them past hope of help. The scene in the court of Mahā Brahmā, the great Brahma, is perhaps the most gigantic that human humour has ever conceived. Here music alone, the humour of Beethoven's symphonies, perhaps may risk comparison.

To the Buddha naught exists save actualities, eternally fermenting, seething, simmering actualities that melt and dissolve all drosses of definitions in their fiery glow or ever they are able to come to birth.

"The art of demonstration was only evolved as far as the first rudiments." I maintain that every single word in this sentence is false or incorrect. The art of demonstration in the philosophical systems that surged all about the Buddha, was developed to a height it never can reach among us for the simple reason that our speech and our brains have lost the necessary flexibility. One has only to read those great Suttas that I might call the transcendental Suttas, such as the Brahmajāla Sutta of the *Dīgha Nikāya*, in order to see that as well speech as brain with us have become so stiff in mechanical views as to be no longer capable of following up and thinking out all these possibilities, all these species and sub-species of idealistic and materialistic views. But it is just for this reason that the Buddha is called the "Master-guide." Like the guide in the catacombs, where at every step the unacquainted are threatened with irretrievable errors, calmly and surely he takes his way through this wild tangle of method, through this rigid logic of the absurd. Serene and clear he recognizes, perceives, "It is altogether conditioned; it is all of the mind's own devising." Again we have the delicate irony that comes of commanding insight, when in another discourse he says, "There are wise men who call day night, and night day." How could one hit off more aptly certain tendencies of modern science—that astounding faculty it displays for interpreting actuality in accordance with preconceived ideas? All those imposing definitions that for our minds and for the human mind in all ages, have possessed such an intoxicating quality, are only possible where one fabricates artificial cores around which dialectical processes can crystallize, and crystallize out all the more splendidly the more carefully one protects them from the rude shocks of actuality. The loftiness and subtlety of our conceptual constructions is nothing but the water-mark that indicates the height of our ignorance. There is certainly much that is confusing for our thought, brought up as that has been under the sway of Aristotelian logic, to see concepts merge and blend upon whose clear differentiation the logical possibility of the entire system seems to rest—such concepts, for example, as *kamma* and *saṅkhāra*, *kamma* and *viññāna*, *kamma* and *taṇha*, and so forth. It may easily happen that the seeker for truth may suffer shipwreck on such apparent contradictions. But in such case it is with him as with one who is stranded on the lighthouse itself—blinded by its very light!

To be able to follow the Buddha here, one must have understood him. What Jesus said of himself in terms of emotion, that, but in terms of understanding, the Buddha also can say, "Blessed is he that is not offended in me."

So long as one continues to take the concepts with which he is operating for positive, firmly established realities, so long is it quite impossible to avoid all these violations of exact thinking. It is said, "If Sañkhāra is the process, it cannot be the energy itself, and *vice versa*." One insists, like the countryman, upon getting one's bill, and has the feeling of intellectual superiority into the bargain.

But there is this to be considered: When, for instance, I wish to define a combustion process, I am at liberty to do so just as it happens to occur to me, either as light, or as heat, or as chemical action, and so forth. On each such occasion I include the whole combustion process in its entirety, and yet none will say, "If the combustion process is at any one time light, it cannot also be heat, for in that case light and heat would be just the same thing. That would be a violation of the law of contradictories," "argal" . . . as the grave-digger in *Hamlet* says. But such grave-digger's logic is followed out in every particular by exact thought when it deals with actuality. It is the pure content of actuality in the Buddha's teaching that renders it irreconcilable with logic. That teaching is not illogical, but simply a-logical. The model of the syllogism does not apply to it at all. For even thus are things in actuality: What at one moment one thinks to have grasped, comprehended, that, next moment, is swept away in the never resting flow of Becoming. Actuality does not play a game that complies with the established rules and regulations called logic: one game only does it play—the grim game of necessity. And this game may be won, not by him who with abstract fences and walls and dykes for a brief space fashions to himself a little world-garden of his own, but only by him who dares to vibrate in unison with the iron rhythm of a beginningless necessity.

It is the indispensable task of every earnest thinker who would really follow the Buddha, experience him in himself, to make clear to himself, and ever and again make clear, that our whole mental life, our concept-world is based upon artificial premisses, in which, in the strictest sense of the words, not life must serve truth but truth life. As the spider itself flings forth its web over the abyss, so from out ourselves we fling forth in the form of concepts an inextricable network of airy roots. As the ape from bough to bough, so springs the human mind from concept to concept, and has itself borne aloft by the entire network, where any single thread would rend beneath him, each individual bough snap under him and precipitate him into the bottomless gulfs of an endless infinitude. All that circulates in daily life in the way of mental values are pure concept-values, bills of exchange upon actuality. But in the hurry and bustle of traffic no one has time or inclination to go and get these bills turned into actual currency. Just as they stand they are passed along "like a basket from hand to hand." Hence the terrible predominance of ideals, the tyranny they exercise over our minds, and so over genuine education and culture. Whoso has experienced in himself the collapse of ideals, the taking up of the bills of current concept-values at the counter of actuality,—he well understands why the Buddha calls his intuition an "awakening." It is the awakening out of the dream-world of concepts.

A Buddha, in short, is a man who dares to *live* this his insight that there are no concepts and accordingly nothing conceived, but only a "conceiving." Hence his attitude towards many questions, and above all to that question as to how one ought to picture to oneself a Buddha, or one who after this life is re-born no more.

The scheme of the questions runs thus: 1. Where is he re-born? 2. Is he not re-born? 3. Is he re-born as well as not re-born? 4. Is he neither re-born nor yet not re-born?

To all these sophistical questions the stereotyped answer of the Buddha is, "That does not apply"—an answer, naturally, which gives plenty of scope for the profoundest conjectures and hypotheses, but which only means that the question is wrongly put and therefore renders impossible any answer at all. A being that with this as his last existence, is proceeding towards extinction, that will never again be re-born *is no longer existent*, even in the form of concept; hence the whole question is meaningless.

Here, again, it is impossible to do anything like justice to the whole problem with the chess-moves of a profound play of thought: only a witticism meets the case. All this ingenious logic that would fain take the measure of actuality with the laws of identity and contradictories as with some yard-stick, which advances against truth with the apparently irresistible demonstrating force of its "aut . . . aut," resembles nothing so much as those ingenious questions with which the child is wont to tease the grown-up person as to the nature and dwelling-place of Santa Claus. Another child would be able to answer these questions with an equal ingenuity; the grown-up person is powerless to meet them. In the same way the scholars of the west would be perfectly capable of meeting and satisfying the questions of a Vacchagotta with equal "acuteness of logic." The Buddha cannot do it. All he can do is to try to sweep away the accumulated rubbish of misunderstood concepts, and on the thus cleared foundation, cause a new clean structure of thought to arise, the essence whereof resides in comprehending that such a thing as the foregoing question refers to has no existence, neither abstractly nor actually; hence, that the question is in itself devoid of meaning.

This is the whole secret here lying hidden. The interpretation given by Oldenburg to the words of the nun Khemā, are based upon a complete misunderstanding of the entire Buddha-thought, as is everything else he says concerning the final goal of Buddhism. But that pertains properly to the Nibbāna teaching.

Buddhism is the doctrine of actuality, and its value as a view of the world from the standpoint of epistemology, lies in the fact that it teaches us to accept actuality as actuality. To this idea it is itself a martyr, inasmuch as its own teaching here is nothing ideally fixed and fast, but only an incitation to experience it in one's own self; it is "a raft, designed for escape; not designed for retention." Hence, is it said in the powerful

Dhātuvibhañga Sutta — Sutta CXL., *Majjhima Nikāya*—"'I am,' monk, is a believing. 'Such am I,' is a believing. 'I shall be,' is a believing. 'I shall not be,' is a believing. 'I shall have a form,' is a believing. 'I shall be formless,' is a believing. 'I shall have perception,' is a believing. 'I shall be devoid of perception,' is a believing. To entertain believings is to be ill. To entertain believings is to be infirm. To entertain believings is to be sick. When, however, all entertaining of believings is overcome, then is one called a right thinker."

And now it may be objected :—

"If there are no concepts, *i.e.* things conceived, at all, but only an individual conceiving, an external, self-renewing reaction to the external world, how is the possibility of our various experiences to be explained?"

To this the reply is :—

Experiences, as understood in the vulgar sense, there are none whatever. Our perceptions are purely token-values out of which experiences may be derived in the same way that practical results may be derived out of a sum of algebraical token-values by cancelling out one against the other. Here must be borne in mind what was treated of in our sixth Essay. With the perception "green" I get no positive content of knowledge, but merely the fact "not-red, not-yellow, not-blue," and so forth.

At this point we are confronted by the so-called epistemological problem, to the which, therefore, we now must devote some little attention.

The question which forms the subject-matter of this problem is this: How is it possible from bare perceptions, mere sense-impressions, ever to arrive at conscious ideas, concepts, experiences?

This problem is associated above all with the name of Kant.

Starting with the idea that the sense-impressions received from without, contain no element out of which experience, *i.e.* an inner connection of individual impressions, could ever be developed, he taught that in the subject there was contained a business capital, so to speak, which, given *a priori* to all experience, upon the occasion of the activity of the organs of sense, came to fruition. This business capital he called the given *a priori* faculty of cognition.

The practical significance of this teaching lies not so much in itself as in the fact that in contrast to it the position of the natural sciences is formulated all the more clearly and distinctly: the passage from bare perceptions to experience is of a purely empirical nature.

The erroneous features in such ideas find some support in certain misunderstood physiological and pathological facts.

Physiology teaches that the human infant does not "see" but only "looks," *i.e.* he is the percipient of impressions from without in virtue of the existence of sense organs, but he attaches no meaning to these impressions. It is the same with the grown-up person after certain lesions of the cerebral cortex, in animals from which the brain has been artificially removed, and so forth. From this the conclusion is drawn that bare perceptions may be transmuted into experiences and that the condition of experience can again sink back into a condition of bare perception.

Such ideas are supported by the teachings of many philosophers who make the young living being to enter the world as a *tabula rasa*, so to speak—as an empty pot which only now is to be filled with material from this world.

All such ideas of the existence of bare perceptions, apart from any content of experience, are based upon a misuse of the word "perception." The infant has no "perceptions." He "experiences" under the circumstances and antecedent conditions proper to himself. It is only we, the adult, who, looking back, can speak of the existence of bare perceptions at this stage, somewhat as, looking back, we can record of Cæsar's Commentaries: "Written in the year so and so before Christ." Wherever there are perceptions, a certain content of experience also is always present, were it only this, that with respect to any definite perception one has no experience at all! To separate perception from experience and then pose the question: "How can pure perceptions pass into experience?" is the same as to separate shell from kernel and then ask, "How can the kernel ever get into the shell?"

The truth is this: The kernel cannot get into the shell at all; both alike are the outcome of a single process of growth. And in the selfsame way experience cannot get into the perceptions at all; both alike are the outcome of a single process of growth. We learn to experience as the flame learns to burn, the flower to blow. We can do nothing save "conceive," lay hold of the outer world. Experiences, as imagined in vulgar thought, there are not. Such would be "concepts," and where there are "concepts" there must be "things conceived." Where these are, there must be identities. Where there are identities, there can be no processes. Where there are no processes, there can be no actuality.

All that we call experience is, so to speak, of the nature of a parallax. Otherwise put: All our knowledge is only the expression of our ignorance. I can say of anything that I know it, only as set off against the total mass of all that I do not know. An *actual* experience would require that I should be able to prognosticate something with *unconditioned* exactitude.

It may further be objected :—

If there are no actual experiences, how can I ever come to have this experience—that there are no experiences? For if it also is no actual experience it has no value. If, on the other hand, it is an actual experience, how is such a thing possible?

The answer is :—

Through an intuitive comprehension of my own self, whereto I receive the inciting impulse from the Buddha-teaching.

With this, we come to the final objection :—

"If there are no concepts, what then is that as which I conceive myself?" In plain words, we are now confronted by that pivot and pole of all thinking—What is self-consciousness?

On the problem of self-consciousness, a teaching is compelled to show whether it is actual or not.

For nothing in the world has sense and meaning in itself, but acquires such only through its relation to me, only from out of self-consciousness.

To the question, "What is self-consciousness?" the answer given is, "Consciousness of oneself." That, however, is an answer which in subtlety and ambiguity outdoes every utterance of the Pythian oracle. For it may just as well mean, "The consciousness of a self in me"—the expression of a pure absolute—as, "The consciousness conscious of itself"—the expression of a pure relative. Self-consciousness is the oracle of nature. Faith interprets this oracle in the former sense; science in the latter.

Therewith, however, both are at odds with themselves. For a pure absolute that becomes conscious of itself, that enters into relation with itself, is an absolute no longer. And a pure relative that enters into relations with itself is equally no longer a pure relative.

"Transcending these two opposites the Tathāgata points out the Truth in the Mean."

Is there any mean here betwixt these opposites?

A wandering monk asks the Buddha :—

"How is it, Gotama? Is there an *I*?"—an Atta, self, as identical with itself.

The Buddha remains silent. The other continues his question :—

"How is it, Gotama? Is there not an *I*?"

The Buddha still maintains silence, and the other goes his way.

If one does not understand the Buddha, it is impossible to interpret this colloquy other than does Oldenburg, for example, in his *Buddha.*

But the meaning is quite otherwise than as there given. We here stand before that which from the standpoint of epistemology constitutes the keystone of the whole Buddha-thought. To understand it fully, we must take a plunge into the heart of modern physics.

One of the most important forward steps taken by physics—if not technically, perhaps, yet easily the most important epistemologically—is its insight in the domain of interference phenomena, especially in the examples of the same afforded by light. A ray of light reflected back upon itself interferes with itself, *i.e.* it forms in itself "stationary waves" which present light as "non-light."

To this paradoxical mode of expression, however, one is only compelled so long as one identifies light with the energy itself. For the site of interference, the nodal point of the vibrations, is just as much "energy" as is the trough of the vibration. And so if one assumes light itself to be the energy, one here has a light without light. In truth, however, light is nothing but an expression of the energy in virtue of which it exists, and it is a stroke of genius on the part of modern physics—one, to be sure, which it has perpetrated unknown to itself—that in interference it has lighted on the one single possibility of making energies perceptible to sense in that one form in which alone they are capable of being made sense-perceptible—*as a pure negative*, a pure *privation* in the sense-activity of me the observer. As all languages become alike in silence, so all energies become alike in interferences. As silence only means that there are languages, so interference only means that there are energies.

With the fact "interference," accordingly, science bears witness against herself, inasmuch as thereby she brings before our eyes the existence of actual energies in the form of the negative itself. That is why I have just called the phenomena of interference the most important step epistemologically that modern physics has yet taken. For if science would but recognize this fact for that which it really is, she would find herself obliged to remodel her whole scheme of thought from the foundation upward.

The—for the beholder—purely negative character of the interference has its basis in the entry of the energy into itself. With this we stand in presence of the Buddha-thought.

Here the fact "self-consciousness" becomes a pure interference phenomenon of *I*-energy. As such it is a pure entering of the *I*-energy into itself. As such, again, it is, on the one hand, a pure negative for the whole external world; on the other hand, to the individual himself, it is a something *immediately* given, where it is simply a matter for correct interpretation, and that, here, in an immediately given, perforce can only be intuitive.

In this insight into the nature of self-consciousness, the *I*, more sharply than anywhere else, defines itself as a something that only comprehends itself, while at the same time comprehending the world as being incomprehensible. In this insight the silence of the Buddha in the face of Vacchagotta's questions explains itself. For, as long as the *terminus technicus* "interference" is not formulated, the question is unanswerable. An interference at once is and is not. It is the immediately given for the individual himself—the not given at all for others, for beholders.

The acceptance and elaboration of this thought is facilitated by the data of physiology and psychology.

The entire course of man's development is to be apprehended as a surging back by degrees upon himself, a "re-flecting" in the most literal sense of the word. Man is the "reflecting" living being, the word being understood as well in its physical as in its psychical sense. The whole process of development from infant to adult is a gradual becoming acquainted with himself. Disgust, shame, are as yet unknown to the infant. These are evolved only as phenomena of "reflection," as a wave of experience running back upon the individual himself, and finding its conclusion in the matured self-consciousness. This self, however, is the stationary wave; at every moment the same and yet another; the—for me—*immediately certain*, as which it presents itself in consciousness; the—for others—not present at all.

In the foregoing it has been shown that both these varieties of attempts at world-conceptions, as well that based upon the concept of *substans* as that which takes the whole play of world-events for pure relation-values, thereby deprive their own selves of the possibility of existence, since from both points of view a world of concepts never could come to be. The Buddha solves the problem by pointing out that there is no such thing as a world of concepts; in the *I*-world, however, the world itself and the world *as such*—the real world and the world of ideation—merge into one in the interference "self-consciousness." And this is the answer to the question, "How must the world be fashioned to render possible the fact that it is present *as such*?"

The insight into the essential nature of self-consciousness is *the* intuition.

The value of an intuition is to be judged by what it accomplishes as a working hypothesis.

What does the Buddha-thought accomplish here?

The answer is:—

It clears up the whole relationship of mental life towards the concept of *substans*.

Every consistent application of the laws of thought seems perforce to conduct to an "unconditioned constant" situated at the root of things, lying, however, beyond all possibility of demonstration.

In this matter three positions are conceivable:—

1. The position of faith which sees in this the proof of an imperceptible to sense in itself—an absolute.

2. The position of science which sees in this a consequence of the imaginative faculty. Its ally is philosophical scepticism—or rather, criticism, chiefly as represented by Hume.

3. That position formulated by Kant with his "thing in itself," which may be briefly characterized as a position of the most resolute indifference towards this most important of all epistemological phenomena. When in his *History of Materialism*, Lange, in agreement with Kant, says: "What right have we to occupy ourselves with 'things in themselves' at all?" this simply means, "What right have we to think at all?" By this stroke,

which Kant carried out by the formulation of his "thing in itself," he has proved himself one of the most hurtful of all noxious creatures found on the tree of the mental life of humanity. Here he has done as much harm as scholastic obtuseness only can do when it steps forth in the polished, mirror-clear armour of a complete logic. But this is not the place to enter any further into that matter.

Upon all these three possibilities the Buddha sheds a simultaneous flood of light, illuminating sceptical criticism especially, in the most exceptional manner.

This latter proves in entirely incontestable fashion that a *substans* seated at the root of things has no existence, yet all its proving possesses not the slightest conclusiveness. Hume, with all his acuteness, falls completely under that paradigm given by R. Avenarius in his *Kritik der reinen Erfahrung*, where a savage contends with a missionary as to whether or no a spirit inhabits in all things. The (unbelieving) missionary is made to say, "I have investigated all these things and never anywhere have I found the spirit." To which the savage counters, "I have investigated them all too, and never anywhere have I failed to find the spirit." Indeed, this example admits of being extended thus far in that the savage must feel himself reinforced in his notion of an immaterial *substans* by the very fact that the other, despite all his search, has found nothing. He would say, "Just *because* you have found nothing, therefore I am right!"

Like the two opposing views of the world,

criticism also operates with a contradiction of itself. To be consistent, the criticism of Hume, as every criticism, ought to run somewhat as follows:—

"A *substans* in things is not demonstrable; these present themselves to me only as a bundle of relation-values. If there is no *substans* in things, how comes it that the idea of a *substans* finds a place in me? Through experience? That, here, were a contradiction in itself; for this idea exists in me, the critic, only in so far as I deny its existence. Consequently there must be something given in me which supplies the foundation for this idea. But I can unravel myself also, to the very last thread and here, too, find nothing but a bundle of relation-values. The one thing in this bundle which I cannot embrace in my comprehension, is this my own capacity of unravelling myself, *i.e.* my consciousness. On this, consequently, I must in fairness withhold myself from passing any judgment."

With this, thought would have so prepared itself —so far as such a thing is possible from its own resources—as to be able to take up and work out the Buddha-thought as inciting impulsion.

From this point the Buddha-teaching, put briefly, would continue:—

All human thinking, without exception, operates with the concept of a *substans* lying at the root of things. Thou also, the critic, must conform thyself to the rule. It is a *necessity of thought*. The ground of this is, that in point of fact a *substans* does lurk in things; not as a "constant in itself," however,—such a thing, to be sure, thou canst through thy rigid analysis exclude—but solely as *that which gives the continuity of the process*, its maintenance, as an *actual* law of formation. This law of formation *becomes* accessible to thee, the individual, in consciousness. To see into that, however, thou must be taught. So long as that does not come to pass, it is a matter of taste or of natural inclination as to whether thou wilt interpret the facts accessible to sense as significant of *substans*, or of the absence of *substans*. For in the facts themselves there lies nothing that impels either in the one direction or the other. The decision lies solely with that unique something *by means of which* you bring all these facts before yourself—namely, with consciousness. To bring this itself before you, however, as a "fact," this is as impossible as that any one should be able to bring his back before him though he should turn himself about never so swiftly and dexterously. To comprehend this unique something—for this, instruction is needed; and following upon this instruction, *growing insight* (intuition). If, however, thou wilt permit thyself to be instructed, then shalt thou learn that both these thought-necessities—that of adequate cause as that of *substans*—here merge into one. *The idea of "substans"* here becomes a form of the law of adequate cause. Both necessities of thought—that of adequate cause and that of *substans*—merge and blend into one in the Kamma teaching of the Buddha.

With this the circle is closed; the end interlocks with the beginning. We have discharged our self-imposed task of assigning the Buddha-thought its place in the life of the mind.

Nothing has been said touching the problem

of the freedom of the will, nor on the problem of deity which involves that of immortality.

The former of these is the problem of morality; the latter, the problem of religion. Their due place is in the successor to this volume.

CONCLUSION

It is clear, without further need of demonstration, that with the Kamma teaching of the Buddha there is given the ferment of an actual morality as of an actual religion. A morality and a religion are *actual* when they are functions of cognition.

All morality rests upon selflessness. If selflessness is not to be blind asceticism or equally blind training, it must have a motive.

This is supplied by the Kamma teaching.

For where I apprehend myself as a process that sustains itself through itself, *i.e.* through its volitions, I know that in every moment I myself fashion the next moment, and with this present life, the life that shall follow it. In correct insight I become in the most literal sense the architect of my fate.

From this, selflessness follows as an evident necessity.

All religion consists in the need of looking beyond this life, of relating it to another, a higher. The Kamma teaching reveals to me that it is the succeeding life to which this life "is related."

From this, morality and religion follow as functions of cognition.

One perceives that such a teaching as this perforce involves profound changes in the appraisement of life-values, and along with this, changes in the relations of the individual to his environment, which includes changes in his social relationships.

The perfumed brutality of our civilization has its root in false ideas of the meaning and significance of life, from which results a false appraisement of life-values. We take the symptoms for the things themselves, and are drowned in their inexhaustibility without once being able to win through to ourselves. That we are all steering a wrong course must be finally clear to every thinking man. But since none knows of any remedy this is sought *practically* in a combat with the symptoms—that is, one bails the water out of the sinking craft and forgets to stop the leak; and *theoretically* it is sought in the setting up of all sorts of artificial ideals—that is, in emotion-values.

Neither of these makeshifts is of any avail. Help can only come from thinking, through the acquiring of a correct idea as to the worth of our so-called life-values.

It is just here that the Buddha-thought comes in as teacher, as educator, as revolutioniser of values—in fine, as the *gospel of thought*, and gives a new turn to that terrible, blind "struggle for existence," to which as to some dread mania, we all are subject.

Buddhism is the doctrine of actuality, the Kamma teaching, the outcome of thinking in terms of actuality. To render it accessible to the thinking of the modern man, to make it possible for him to let his glance rove free from out the mole-like existence of aims and objects himself has turned up, away past the overthrown barriers of a cramping ignorance—for this it is necessary that the non-actual and the re-actual forms of world-theory, which, as faith and science respectively, everywhere obstruct free outlook, should be swept clean away, or at the very least confined strictly to their own proper domain. Room must be made for actuality and for thinking in terms of actuality.

That was the main task of this book.

But of such sort is truth that it will not suffer that way be made for it by violent measures of any kind. One thing only here is permissible: to point it out, patiently and repeatedly point it out. Its way it makes of its own self.

"Over all gifts victorious is the gift of the truth."

THE END

Printed by R. & R. CLARK, LIMITED, *Edinburgh*.